# About the author

Born in Glasgow in 1941. Spent teenag years in Crieff and Pitlochry, climbing in Perthshire hills and the Cairngorms. Attended skiing and climbing courses at Glenmore Lodge in the early sixties. Trained as a primary school teacher at Jordanhill from 1960 - 63, then returned to Glasgow in 1965 to join the Langside Mountaineering Training Centre. Has kept diaries and holiday journals since the 1950's and had several mountaineering holidays

in the Dolomites and the Alps from 1965 to 1969. Married John Quinn, member of the Starav Mountaineering Club in Glasgow in 1968.

After moving to Sutherland in 1971 has spent time as a supply teacher as well as twenty five years as a newspaper correspondent with The Northern Times and twelve years as a music instructor in whistle and accordion for youngsters. Has attended creative writing courses, both residential and local and has written a previous book entitled 'Spellbound in the Cairngorms.'

First published in 2017 by
LQ Press
Cnoc Grainach
Main Street
Lairg
IV27 4AR
Tel: 01549 402187

Design and layout by Eilidh Price

A CIP catalogue record for this book is available from the British Library.

ISBN 978-0-9956493-1-6

Printed and bound by Bell & Bain Limited, Thornliebank, Glasgow

By the same author:
*Spellbound in the Cairngorms (2016)*

*Front cover image: Liz in Glencoe, 1963*
*Back cover image: Liz walking into the Matterhorn, 1969*

# SCRAPES
## AND
# SCRAMBLES

Humorous climbing exploits from the
Scottish Highlands to the Alps in the 1960s

## Liz Quinn

## Dedication

To the people I climbed with in the 1960's and who fostered my enthusiasm for the sport, in particular to organisations like Glenmore Lodge in the Cairngorms and the Langside Mountaineering Training Centre in Glasgow, who introduced me to the Dolomites in Italy – also to my college friend Anne with whom I explored the Scottish Highlands and the west in the early sixties and to my husband John, a former member of the Langside who accompanied me on a return trip to the Dolomites in 1967 and to Zermatt and Chamonix in 1969. Finally I would like to thank the Glasgow school children for the pleasure of being able to introduce them to the hills.


## Reasons for writing this book

There was a Golden Age of mountaineering well before the 1960's, when new routes were pioneered and hitherto unclimbed peaks scaled by the early pioneers of the sport, but as far as I am concerned my Golden Age for climbing was in the 1960's. This was an era less than twenty years after the end of World War Two when young people without much money, cars and equipment were flooding to the hills from industrial cities like Glasgow, looking for adventure and freedom. Clubs were springing up and young men, along with a few women, were rushing out of Glasgow on Friday nights with a pack on their backs to hitchhike from Balloch to Glencoe where there was a new world of challenging mountains. Many wilderness areas of the west became favourite haunts, but Glencoe was the epicentre. Basic make-do accommodation was procured in barns and huts, where club members installed wood burning stoves and Alpine sleeping shelves, while others were prepared to doss anywhere there was shelter from the elements, including under bridges and boulders on the hillside, a famous howff of this nature being on the Cobbler path at Arrochar.

It was an era not to be missed, when people put up with basic facilities, spent their days climbing in the hills and their nights singing to the twang of guitars in draughty dosses. That era has all but gone. Modern technology, equipment and fast cars have taken over – and even in the Alps I hear there are changes of a different nature, as I believe that global warming has reduced the once brilliant and expansive glaciers to a fraction of their previous glory, including the majestic Gorner Glacier above Zermatt and Chamonix's acclaimed Mer de Glace, while much of the summer snow on the huge faces of the Matterhorn is also reported to be disappearing.

I'm glad I was a climber in the sixties and I hope to convey what this charismatic era was like in this collection of humorous stories concerning bothies, dosses, emergency howffs, hitchhiking, climbing experiences, weekending, Alpine huts and some of the great Alpine peaks, the fantastic Dolomite towers and thunderstorms – and introducing young Glasgow school children to the adventure on their doorstep.

# Contents

## Preface by Dave Brown from Glasgow, co author with Ian Mitchell for "Mountain Days and Bothy Nights" published in 1987

The 1960's was a period of great change in approaches to Scottish mountains. The influence of working class climbers and walkers introduced a new way of going to the hills that was called 'weekending'. It focused not only on a climbing style that resulted in rocketing standards, but also referred to how we got to the hills and how we lived when we arrived. It was influenced by the pre war movement of working climbers and walkers such as Jock Nimlin. Although more affluent than Nimlin's generation, there was not much money about. Even if you had money, mountaineering equipment was basic so the leader was not advised to fall.

Although there were club buses that were cheap, people often hitched lifts to climbing areas. Arrival at one's destination was not guaranteed. Once there you either camped, stayed in dosses or bothies. Adherants to the sport went away every weekend, rain, hail or snow, summer and winter. It could be exhilarating or it could be miserable. Numbers were relatively small and you tended to know most others who were involved. There was rivalry between different groups, but there was also a great spirit of community. While they might have been the start of the modern mass movement one sees to the mountains today, at that time they were an odd bunch of outsiders, not always welcome in the hotels, pubs and estates of the Highlands.

The book that Liz has written is a very good description of what it was like to be on the scene at that time, and she does it from the perspective of a female, a species that was not common in the mountains in the sixties. We get the first tentative steps on to the hills when knowledge is minimal and the learning curve is steep. There are setbacks when weather and lack of expertise bring defeats, even down right misery, but eventually there are triumphs, all captured in Liz's highly detailed and humorous writing style, informed by her obvious enthusiasm for the subject.

Eventually this enthusiasm sought an outlet in the wider prospects of the Alps. So off we go to the Dolomites and to Switzerland, where although great deeds were planned and bold adventures attempted, they often foundered. This should not put the reader off. Liz and her husband John attempted climbs on such as the Matterhorn and Monte Rosa, at a time when there was not much knowledge of routes and conditions available – something that always made things more difficult, uncertain and hence scary. Along the way we meet some great characters such as the drunk that attached himself to them on their attempt on Monte Antelao in Italy and "Madame" the keeper of the Bahnhof Hotel in Zermatt, Switzerland.

Having been there myself at that time I think Liz and John were quite bold even to attempt the climbs they chose. They were part of a generation that showed that ordinary climbers could actually go to the Alps and seek success there. Numbers on the hills increased over the years, informed by word of mouth, and as they did so, then came the guide books that would make planning trips that could be accomplished much more certain.

This is why Liz's book is important. It gives an insight into a significant historical period as it was experienced by ordinary climbers, before the mysteries were revealed by guide books and the internet, making things so much easier today. They were both at the end of something influenced by the pre-war working class movement, and also at the beginning of something – the mass movement of climbing and walking tourism that we see today.

## Comments from Willie Anderson
## Leader of the Cairngorm Mountain Rescue Team

'Scrapes and Scrambles' follows on from 'Spellbound in the Cairngorms' by Liz. It is quite apparent that her love for the mountains extended beyond Scotland's gems in the Cairngorms and Glencoe. You always got the feeling from 'Spellbound' that further exploration was in her blood.

It would have been considered 'unusual' for a group of girls to go exploring new stomping grounds at that period, but then Liz was clearly a free radical in that respect.

It's easy to glance over the commitment required for trips to the Alps or Dolomites in these days, but on reading this book it's also easy to get a sense of the drive and ambition that Liz had for exploring new and larger pastures in the 1960's.

Scrapes and Scrambles is a diary of her experiences which those of us who have been to these places will have much resonance with. She reflects on many days spent exploring new areas with a light humour of errors, hardships, difficult decisions and chance encounters. I am certain you will get a grasp of 'Liz Quinn, mountaineer', her love of the mountains and all that goes along with her passion for the high tops as you peruse each story in turn.

# Introduction

My first camping holiday in the Scottish Highlands occurred in 1957 when I was fifteen. Having just returned to live in Scotland after ten years in suburban Surrey, my parents decided we would explore the far North with a couple of tents.

My only previous experience of camping had been in the back garden in Surrey and a regimental girl guide camp in the vicinity of Bognor Regis when I was eleven. The week long camp had taken place in a field near the south coast, with bell shaped tents and sleeping bags comprising sewn up blankets. There were early morning patrol inspections, tasks to complete during the day and two afternoons at the nearest beach, walking to the appointed place in an orderly crocodile. Self-expression and exploration were discouraged and transgression of the rules was not tolerated.

I'd never known my parents to camp before our present venture and by this time they were middle aged, so I was surprised at the decision. Two small ridge tents were borrowed for the occasion, along with separate groundsheets and antique fold up canvas beds with metal legs, while father's sister loaned lightweight khaki sleeping bags that looked like surplus ex-army gear from World War Two.

After departure from Crieff in our Standard Ten car that my father had bought to explore the Highlands, we set off up the old A9 from Perth, heading for Inverness and beyond, with our first night being spent in Dornoch on the east coast. It was particularly memorable for an invasion of earwigs, which had bred copiously on the machair that year and were now crawling everywhere inside the tent. Mother declared she was still emptying them out of her handbag a week later!

Our second night was at Dunnet Bay on the north coast. We arrived late in the evening on empty, wind and rain-soaked grasslands backing the beach and erected the tents in close proximity to the road. Tent guys had to be re-secured during the night and in the morning it was still raining,

1

making them wonder if camping had been such a good idea. In this respect night number three was spent in a bed and breakfast in Bettyhill, but after that the weather improved so the tent came out again at an idyllic sandy cove near Durness. However, our halcyon evening was shattered when we spotted a large oil-soaked seabird. It had been swept ashore on the incoming tide and was flapping feebly amongst the rocks. Father declared that nothing could be done and it would have to be dispatched with a large stone to save it from further misery, while I fervently opposed the solution and repaired to my tent, tying the door flaps tight.

The camping holiday had not been much of a success so far and the great outdoors with interesting mountains to explore had so far not manifested itself. This was because we'd spent two days driving through Caithness which was flat, but things were looking up the next day when we turned down the west coast and I caught sight of the craggy mountains of Beinn Spionnaidh and Cranstackie, as we motored down the twisting single track road towards Foinaven and Laxford Bridge. Father meanwhile was meandering slowly along the road in the brilliant sunshine prevailing above, and unfortunately a string of traffic was building up behind us, tooting impatiently to get past.

"For goodness sake Archie," my mother implored him. "Pull over and let these people pass." But father chose to ignore them saying, "People are in far too much of a hurry these days."

The tooting became louder and more persistent, while I shrank into the back seat, too embarrassed to turn round and see if angry faces and fingers were pointing crossly in my direction, as if I was to blame for this inconvenience.

When they got past eventually the horn blowing escalated, letting us know that we had transgressed the rules of the single track road, but father's answer to that was his own crescendo of tooting, while mother and I cringed. She was red-faced and cross, while I silently prayed that no more traffic would catch us up from behind!

Our next episode was of a different nature altogether and concerned our overnight accommodation. By this time we were in the region of Scourie on Saturday afternoon and father had drawn up at what he thought was a suitable field with a pull-in off the road next to it. They were starting to unload the camping gear when a gentleman appeared on the other side of the dry stone dyke, hay fork in hand, saying, "I hope you're not planning staying here overnight, because if you are, you can't move on until Monday. It's the Sabbath tomorrow you know. Nobody moves on the Sabbath, except to church."

"In that case," says father bristling, "we won't be staying. No one tells me what to do on my summer holidays!"

With that the tents were thrown back into the boot, the lid slammed shut and we carried on towards Lochinver, taking a narrow, perpendicular and twisting route along the coast from Kylesku, via Drumbeg and Clashnessie. We found a spot near the latter - a quarry hole at the foot of a cliff, with the sea just yards away across the road. Unfortunately it rained all night and I could hear water splashing down the cliff behind us, as well as the sea encroaching in front on the incoming tide, sounding alarmingly close.

So much for our scenic tour of the west which had been marked with incidents, more than scenery, but the best was still to come as we motored into Lochinver and saw Suilven rising like a sentinel from the moors, surrounded by sheer impregnable looking cliffs. The image of it was one of those stunning unforgettable moments – one day I was determined to stand at the top?

The following year we went to Skye as described in my previous book entitled 'Spellbound,' and in 1959 I discovered the magic of the Cairngorms and Glenmore Lodge.

It was 1963 before I was able to fully explore the west coast and this was done with a college friend called Anne.

# PART 1: ANNE 1963-64

# 1

# SPOOKED IN TORRIDON

My early hill walking was done in Perthshire and the Cairngorms between 1956 and 1962, either alone, with Glenmore Lodge or with various boyfriends, apart from a trek through the Lairig Ghru with an old school friend from London and another with the geography teacher from Pitlochry High School. While I was at college in Glasgow I was on the lookout for a more permanent climbing companion and in my third year I found Anne. Our association only lasted a couple of years, but unbeknown to me at the time she was to shape the rest of my life.

I found her through a scribbled message on the college notice board. It was advertising for new members for the Glenmore Mountaineering Club, signed Anne, with a phone number in brackets underneath. I took the number down on the back of a bus ticket and when I returned to my hall of residence at night I queued at the pay phone. Anne answered the call and immediately dispelled two illusions. One, it was nothing to do with my old haunt at Glenmore Lodge, and two, she didn't seem to be particularly involved with the said club – despite being interested in climbing.

We made an arrangement to meet the following day and hit it off to such an extent that we made plans to have an Easter holiday together in Torridon. Neither of us had ever been there, but it was far away on the north west coast and promised excellent climbing on high rugged peaks. It was beyond Glencoe and Ben Nevis and further north than the road to Skye, but not as far as the trail I had once done with my parents in 1957. It was to be a real adventure and would not entail staying in bothies, because Anne had a tent, not an old cumbersome girl guide tent like the one my parents had used, but a proper mountaineering job, an Andre Jamet model for one person with sewn in groundsheet and flysheet. Anne said it would stretch to two persons, and I agreed to provide the climbing rope, belay slings and Karabiners.

We discussed the matter endlessly and it became more important than our forthcoming final exams at college, apart from psychology which was taking place immediately after the Easter break and prompted us to take our 'Valentines Psychology and it's bearing on Education' tomes with us for revision on wet days - these additions significantly adding to the weight of our already overloaded packs.

We started hitching up the A9 from Pitlochry, leaning our packs on top of a fence to relieve the weight, but it wasn't long before a grain lorry stopped and we gained considerable respect from the driver as he helped to haul our packs into the cab! It was a long, slow lift over the Drumochter Pass to Inverness on the old A9 and conversation was curtailed due to noisy vibration from the engine. By the time he dropped us off in the Highland capital our ears were buzzing and our voices hoarse with shouting. It was a relief to secure our next uplift in a smart saloon car, with a golf enthusiast who whisked us round the Beauly Firth to Muir of Ord, but after that we were downgraded again into a shabby grey van owned by a plumber, where we exchanged perfumed upholstery for the odour of pipes and putty. The driver jogged and squeaked along towards the west, prattling on about his plumbing jobs and social life and eventually dropping us at Garve, where there was a road junction for Ullapool to the North and Achnasheen in the west, which was the route we wanted to take.

By this time it was getting dark and traffic had dwindled, with most vehicles turning off towards Ullapool. We passed the time with guessing games, scoring points for correct answers, until an argument developed on the accuracy of certain geographical locations, which was fortunately saved from escalation by the appearance of a Land Rover heading in our direction. It stopped in response to our energetic thumbing and the driver jumped out, unlatched the rear door and invited us to squeeze into the back where another couple of men were already sitting in overalls and wellingtons, smelling of earth and trees. We deduced they were forestry workers and as the driver had already told us he was headed to Shieldaig on the west coast, this would be our last lift. His route was through Torridon Glen where we planned to camp, between two of the region's highest mountains, Beinn Eighe and Liathach. We'd studied the area on a one inch map. It was remote, lonely and perpendicular, considerably attractive to adventurers like ourselves, but we didn't know at the time that our biggest adventure was not going to involve climbing!

After passing the small hamlet of Kinlochewe we reminded the driver where we wanted to be dropped off. "You sure?" he said. "It's still winter up here you know. Wouldn't you be better going on to the village."

"No," Anne replied. "This is closer to the hills we want to climb."

The driver clicked his tongue in disapproval, while our companions in the back muttered 'mad' under their breath. Fortunately he stopped as requested and waited as we hauled our packs out onto the darkened verge before departing with exaggerated exhaust, telling it's own tale of what the locals thought of our plans, as his headlights disappeared into the darkness.

We snapped on our head torches and set off uphill through deep heather sprinkled with boulders, searching for a flat enough area to pitch the tent. A high wall loomed ahead, but it turned out to be a dry stone dyke and we heard the sound of rushing water nearby. There was a flattish area on the far side so we set about crossing the stream which was reasonably shallow with stepping stones. Anne reached the opposite bank unscathed, but one of my stepping stones wobbled and the weight of my pack unbalanced me, resulting in an involuntary sit down in the water! Anne dropped her pack in the heather and came to my assistance, trying to pull me up, but she slipped too, leaving us both floundering in the stream. That was a fine end to our day's travelling and the start of the holiday, but all we could do was laugh, while I couldn't help thinking that the forestry boys were probably right in their description of our plans.

Once inside the tent with dry clothes on and the remains of the day's sandwiches we studied our map with a torch. We had our rope, belay lengths and ice axes and we hoped to make grand ascents of the mountains behind us. We were going to be pioneers in this remote and desolate area. Well that was the plan!

The following morning we wakened to brilliant sunshine and cloudless skies, but we were completely overwhelmed by the scale of the peaks towering above, still with a mantle of snow on the tops and seriously perpendicular. There was no hurry for our possible conquests as we had a whole week in front of us so we decided to spend the day reconnoitring.

One thing we hadn't expected was the complete isolation, lack of human activity and habitation. The glen was eerily silent, apart from an odd car that trundled along the road towards the coast. Our two earmarked peaks frowned down on us behind our camp, and in front, across the road we suddenly became aware that there was an isolated cottage almost blending into the muted background near Lochan an Iasgaich. We decided to investigate it, but it was almost certainly uninhabited.

A water-logged footpath led across the moor to the said building, but as we suspected there was no sign of habitation. We circled the property and looked in the dusty windows, suddenly feeling we had to revise our previous assumption that it was uninhabited. There were tables and chairs, books and mountaineering tackle hanging from a row of pegs. Was it a bothy? The front door was locked, but as we raked about I fell over an upturned pail and beneath it was a key! "Look what I've found," I shouted to Anne. We tried it in the lock and the door opened.

As the premises were presently unoccupied, we sat down in two camp chairs at the table, relishing the satisfaction of a proper seat after crawling about the Andre Jamet midget tent. There was a log book on the table so we flicked through the pages and realised immediately that we were in a private mountaineering club premises called 'The Ling Hut' owned by the prestigious Scottish Mountaineering Club known as the SMC. We felt a bit guilty, but nevertheless we rustled through the pages of the log to see if we could find any information about routes, but there was nothing of much use to us, in our raw inexperience of the area's impressive peaks.

We closed the book and vacated the hut, locking the door behind us and replacing the key under the bucket. Our next bright idea was to take a walk in the opposite direction along the road to the village which was about five miles away and would take us along the length of Liathach. There seemed to be no feasible route of access that didn't involve superior equipment to tackle it, but we reckoned a route might be found to the rear and resolved to try this approach the following day.

The village when we arrived bore little sign of life. Nobody walked in the street and grey stone houses nestled under the brooding cliffs, with wisps of smoke curling from a few chimneys. We turned around and walked back to our camp site where we made a meal from the contents of tins and packets, polished off with Penguin biscuits for desert. Anne had a friend who worked in MacDonald's Chocolate Biscuit factory in Glasgow and she had provided us with three dozen unwrapped Penguin biscuits for our holiday. They were rapidly becoming our staple pudding desert!

The next day our grand plans were abandoned when we found it was drizzling rain and the peaks were completely obliterated in thick mist. We could see it was on for the day and although the rain was not heavy it was persistent. We spent the morning at camp reading our psychology books and in the afternoon, with the drizzle dispersing but the mist stubbornly refusing to shift, we decided on a walk to restore the circulation. Three miles up the glen towards Kinlochewe there was a track branching off the road on our right which followed the banks of Loch Clair into the forest, past Coulin Lodge and on towards Loch Coulin.

The atmosphere was strangely quiet and subdued as we marched along, and fingers of low mist were drifting lazily along the surface of

Loch Clair creating a sensation of creepiness. In the forest a gloom also descended and as we approached the lodge the silence was suddenly broken by a long wailing howl. We stopped talking and listened with a shiver as the howl faded into the distance. "Was that a dog?" I said without any degree of conviction. We couldn't be sure. Then it came again even more mournful than before. Was it a wild animal caught in a trap? We shivered at the thought. I looked up into the branches of the trees and jumped as I caught sight of an animal skin hanging above our heads. It looked like a deer skin, but we couldn't tell how old it was. We quickened our pace to try and clear the wood before the lodge buildings appeared ahead of us. Maybe there were kennels behind them?

Our track passed close by the lodge which seemed to be unoccupied and as we glanced over to the windows we noticed the furniture within was shrouded in white dust sheets. This did nothing for morale as the shadowy shapes assumed the appearance of ghosts.

We hurried on towards Loch Coulin where the walk opened out, although the forest persisted on our right - and here things unexpectedly took a turn for the worse. I was aware of a soft sighing in the long damp grass beneath the trees. It seemed to come in waves through the stillness, a huffing, sloughing sigh, gently repeating itself as if something was waiting to pounce. The hackles rose on my neck as I felt an invisible presence of someone watching us. It was like a late night horror film accompanied by electrifying tension. I was reluctant to turn round and peer into the undergrowth and as we walked it also became more difficult to continue, like something was stopping us, pushing us back. I looked at Anne and it was obvious she had also been affected.

Simultaneously we both whirled round and started running back towards the lodge and Loch Clair, our breath coming in long uneven pants. We knew we had to pass the lodge and as we drew near the darkened shadowy windows I felt drawn to snatch a glance, where all the white wreathed shapes now seemed to be dancing and mocking us as we streaked past. Was it just shadows and a trick of the light against the glass? Then in the background the long mournful, echoing howl wailed interminably, while fingers of wraith like mist slid like stealthy, hissing snakes, weaving a pattern between the trees and across the water. We didn't stop running until we saw the glen road ahead of us and just as we emerged onto tar macadam we saw a notice nailed to a post that we hadn't been aware of before. It said 'Beware wild cats!'

"Was that weird howl from a cat?" I said, trying to steady my breathing.

None of us could explain our strange experience, but by the time we'd regained our camp and were reclining snugly inside our Lilliputian home our composure had returned and we felt angry with ourselves for imagining such ghostly apparitions. Instead of packing up and getting the hell out of the place we chastised ourselves for letting the possibility of a supernatural presence unnerve us and we were considerably ashamed. After all we called ourselves mountaineers and we'd been in the glen for two days and achieved nothing. Tomorrow we resolved was going to change all that.

The weather was fine in the morning so we lost no time in gathering our mountaineering equipment and setting off on a faint path through the heather which seemed to lead up between the two mountains. Our plan was to tackle one of them from the rear. The closer we came to our objectives the more intimidating they became and with the upper slopes plastered in snow this didn't exactly help matters. Even from behind they were not much better.

Liathach was ruled out at once, but we decided to have a go at Beinn Eighe. Here, good progress was made initially until we reached the snow line, after which we were much more cautious. The slope was steepening dramatically and we were not sure if rock, scree or vegetation lay below the snow cover. It seemed to go up in ledges and having reached one of these we were undecided whether to go on. Without crampons we were cutting steps with our axes and some of them were not holding where the snow was insecure, leading to some risky slides, not to mention all this would have to be reversed when and if we reached the summit. Without proper knowledge of the mountain ahead we decided to retreat and try a different route further round the back, but when we tried to climb down we found we were stuck. After all my Glenmore Lodge experience I was quite ashamed to have arrived in this position. Part of our insecurity came from the desolate nature of the region, and not having seen anyone else since we'd arrived - but eventually we took the plunge and kicked steps back down, keeping our axes ready to break any unexpected glissade.

Having regained the pass we decided we'd wasted too much time to start trying for another route that day. Our point scoring was abysmal – three days gone – score nil – three to go.

Day number four was a virtual downpour in the valley with escalating wind which prevented us from lighting our primus stove outside. We had Penguin biscuits for breakfast and passed the time singing over all the folk lyrics in Anne's song book. By midday all the remaining dry corners of the tent interior were wet and our sleeping bags were in danger of being soaked too, as water dripped from the flysheet onto the inner tent and finished up on the floor. There was no sign of any improvement and we were sick of Penguin biscuits so we reluctantly decided to pack up and head for the youth hostel in Glencoe.

We hadn't exactly been welcomed in this lonely outpost we grumbled as we packed. Spooks, battering rain, impenetrable mist, gales and inaccessible icy mountains all seemed to have gathered forces to evict us! Whether we were even going to get a lift out of the place was a debatable issue.

In later years I returned to Torridon on several occasions with different people, climbing both Liathach and Beinn Eighe and on the last occasion I was there in the summer of 2012 we arrived in the middle of a triathlon with competitors in their hoards sprinting up Beinn Eighe, swimming across Loch Torridon and pedalling furiously on push bikes in both directions along the road. Parking spaces were limited and there was a sparkling new community centre in the village with badminton halls, fitness suite, tea shop and library, while further along the road there were craft shops and a restaurant. What a transformation!

But one thing I have never done in subsequent visits is to return to Loch Coulin!

Moving back again fifty years we were now packed and ready to leave, and much to our surprise a solitary car splashed up the hostile glen and offered us a lift to Kinlochewe. The driver was a local west coast man, up for a chat, so we regaled him with our escapades in the area. When we started on the spooks we had encountered an amused smile played about his lips, but he was reticent on the matter, so we never did get to the bottom of our Glen Coulin ghost.

From Kinlochewe a couple going to Dingwall for their weekly shop dropped us at Contin. They would have taken us right into Dingwall where they said we'd be better placed for lifts to Inverness, but it was ourselves who insisted on getting out at Contin, thinking it was a short cut south to Muir of Ord. Well short cut it might have been if there was any traffic to take us there, but there was nothing apart from the odd tractor and some push bikes. We hung about the junction for nearly two frustrating hours and then as if to add insult to injury we saw the same couple who had dropped us off returning with their shopping. We ducked hastily in embarrassment, then ended up taking a lift to Dingwall after all!

Once back on the A9 we got a lift almost immediately from a delivery lorry carrying rolls of linoleum, along with kitchen and bathroom fittings. The driver asked if we minded small detours to make deliveries, but we were glad of the lift and said "No – not at all." However the detours were between ten and twenty miles off the route and the deliveries were taking so long that we offered to lend a hand. It was the laugh of the day as we marched through farm yards and into rambling country houses, each with a roll of linoleum across one shoulder and tempted to sing, "Hi ho, hi ho, It's off to work we go. We work all day, we get no pay, Hi ho hi ho ho ho ho!"

After all that hilarity it was early evening by the time we reached Inverness and we were becoming dubious about reaching Glencoe Youth Hostel before closing time. However, as the alternative was to re-erect the sodden tent, we pressed on down the Great Glen hoping for the best. A short lift took us to Urquhart Castle on Loch Ness after which further hitching prospects were looking bleak. It was also getting dark and we were hungry. Not wanting to stop for a meal on route in case we missed a lift had reduced us to nibbling on Penguin biscuits all day. After this holiday I didn't think I'd ever again buy a packet of Penguins!

There was a ruined cottage across the road from where we were hitching, but after inspecting it as a prospective doss for the night it got the thumbs down, on account of absent roof and a carpet of stinging nettles. We were saved from this horror by a late night fish lorry that took us to Fort William and another bout of bad weather on the west coast.

We dived into a convenient telephone kiosk to discuss the situation. It was 11pm and the hostel would be closed, but suddenly we heard the rumble of another lorry. We scurried outside and thumbed energetically, sighing with relief when it drew to a creaking halt beside us. We scrambled up into the warmth of the cab, hauling our packs behind us, and the driver, a large, burly, unshaven individual mumbled that he could take us to a timber camp at Onich, where his mate might be able to take us on to Glencoe in his van. This was great news although where we were going to stay when we arrived we had no idea. That particular problem didn't arise however, because when we reached Onich the mate's van was bogged down in a ditch and he was going nowhere.

Midnight in Onich in pitch darkness and drenching rain was an uninviting prospect. There was only one thing to do, which was to start walking, and soon we found ourselves passing a few outlying houses on the way to the centre of Onich. Surprisingly one of them had lights on in the downstairs windows. "I'm going to knock on the door," I said, "and see if they could help us."

"What?" said Anne in alarm, "Not at this time of night."

"It's just a chance," I replied. "We're stuck aren't we? What else can we do?"

Anne stood at the gate while I marched up the path to the front door and rang the bell. I was trying to think up what I was going to say as I waited, then suddenly the front door swung open revealing a middle-aged couple in overalls and dust caps and bringing with them a waft of fresh paint.

I explained our position and they looked at each other, then back at me and over my shoulder where Anne was still hovering guiltily.

"Well to be sure," said the gentleman. "We're just getting rooms ready for the tourist trade, but if you're desperate you could sleep in our summer house round the back. It's where we sleep ourselves when the house is full. It's littered with junk mind, but if you want to shift things around and rough it you could share the bed. Any use?" His eyebrows shot up dubiously.

"That would be wonderful," I said, resisting the temptation to give him a hug.

I signed to Anne and we followed him round to the summer house, which as he had indicated had definitely become a dumping ground during the winter season. Nevertheless, it was dry and there was a bed we could use after we shifted the plumbing fittings, including a white porcelain WC pedestal reclining on top of the mattress. The guy apologised for having to rush back to the house to finish his painting job, but we were ecstatic as we shifted the clutter and hauled our sleeping bags from our packs, before settling down on the comfortable sprung mattress for well earned sleep.

# 2

# EXHILARATION IN GLENCOE

After our night of refreshing sleep in the summer house at Onich we rose early the next morning, replaced the plumbing equipment on the bed and went round to thank the couple for their hospitality.

We were now headed into Glencoe and were lucky to get a lift almost immediately from a grocer's delivery van, trying to keep our eyes off the stack of food it was transporting - tins, packets, bakery items, succulent fresh fruit and vegetables - while we only had Penguin biscuits.

By the time we reached Glencoe it was nearly midday. Our driver dropped us at the door of the luxurious Glencoe Hotel and thinking we deserved a good hot meal after our two days on the road, we marched straight in the front door like a couple of tramps, crumpled jackets, mud splashed trousers and all, and ordered dinner for two at the reception desk. After that we went to the ladies powder room and had a complete blast, letting out shrieks of delight as hot water gushed from the taps, while revelling in the soft carpeted floors in our stocking soles and parading in front of the full length mirror. There was nothing like a few days wild camping and tramping on the road to make one appreciate the comforts of civilization!

We presented ourselves in the immaculate dining room, still in our stocking soles, shirt sleeves rolled above the elbow and jackets draped over one arm, as we tried to slip inconspicuously into a couple of chairs with tartan upholstered seats at our allotted table. Fortunately the folds of the white starched tablecloth concealed our creased trousers, but we were aware of curious stares as other diners, respectable Easter holiday trippers touring the Highlands in their cars, cast surreptitious glances in our direction. We ignored their fleeting attention as we filled our glasses to the brim with cool iced water and ordered a lavish meal from the waitress, who was immaculately attired in black skirt and cardigan, with white lace trimmed apron and cap. We blushed in embarrassment, but when the fare arrived it was the best meal we'd ever tasted!

In the afternoon we walked up the old road to Glencoe Youth Hostel and booked in for the rest of the week. To date I had only ever stayed in one youth hostel which was at Loch Morlich, when I was doing the Lairig Ghru. On that occasion I knew the building because it had been the old Glenmore Lodge during my eventful first skiing course in the Cairngorms. Not long after the war hostels were springing up everywhere, providing cheap accommodation for young adventurers to explore the countryside. Prospective hostellers joined the association, after which they received a card which was stamped for overnight stays, with it becoming a project to see how many different stamps you could collect! At only a few shillings a night the hostels were cheap, but a job had to be done in the morning before leaving, like scrubbing the kitchen pots and pans, washing down the sinks, sweeping the floors or polishing the stairs etc. Kitchen equipment and dishes were provided, along with rows of boxed cubby holes for storing provisions and the dormitories had squeaky bunk beds. Sleeping sheets could also be hired. In the sixties these premises were mostly used by young walkers and climbers who arrived on foot or by bicycle, with a rucksack on their shoulders and lugging a guitar as well, because the hostels were well known for folk singing in the common room in the evenings.

Fifty years on their image has changed. There are places still described as hostels but inside they could be mistaken for hotels, with en-suite twin bedrooms and meals cooked and served in a dining room by resident staff. Visitors generally arrive by car with a suitcase, seldom talk to strangers and community singing in the evening is unlikely! Where our entertainment extras could be a pack of cards, liar dice, sketch pad and pencil, song books or musical instruments, these items now seem to have been replaced by the latest computer technology and indispensable 'do it all' mobile phone. As for the cost, that has rocketed too, although there is one compensation - you don't have to scrub the floor before you leave!

I have to say I was glad I was a hosteller in the sixties before the fun went out the window. We had an excellent time at the Glencoe hostel and as it was full of climbers and hikers there was plenty craic about routes and peaks ascended, and tips passed on about other places worth visiting.

On our first full day in Glencoe we decided to climb the glen's highest peak, Bidean nam Bian at 3,766 feet. Snow was still about half way down from the tops, but we had selected a good access route and were suitably confident. I was already noticing a difference between the west coast climbing areas and the Cairngorms which I'd more or less grown up in. The Cairngorms were far more extensive, keeping their best secrets hidden and requiring a longer walk in, while most of the popular west coast peaks were very accessible from the nearest road. Everything was there in your face as it were, but once conquered, despite the grandeur, it was tempting to move on to other challenges. In the 1960's however, the grandeur of the area as far as I was concerned was just unfolding.

Our ascent of Bidean was via Stob Coire nam Beith above Loch Achtriochtan, after which we had to kick and cut steps in the snow onto the narrow ridge of An-t Sron. We were much bolder in Glencoe than we had been in Torridon, probably due to the fact that the area was much busier and after a night in Glencoe hostel with social contact and banter our confidence was rising.

There had been some mist on the tops when we'd left the glen, but now as we approached the summit of Bidean from the ridge it lifted spectacularly, like a curtain suddenly swept aside to reveal an exhilarating panorama in all directions. It was the view I imagined in the Alps, which up until now I had only seen in photographs. We pulled our cameras out and snapped everything in sight, including each other. We even snapped the Glencoe road far below us, where toy-like cars moved along in both directions, sometimes lost in the shadow of the towering mountains above.

From the summit we took a different route until we arrived at a col above the valley of Allt Coire Gabhail, otherwise known as the lost valley, due to it being hidden from the road below. Up on the col the sun was blazing down, tempting us to take forty winks stretched out on the snow, before beginning the descent over the cornice into the shade of the valley. Clearing the cornice was intimidating, so we roped up and belayed each other as we cut steps in the ice, but everything went to plan and we were soon below the snowline. After our trials in Torridon we were pleased with our accomplishments, even though we found the final exit from the valley an unexpectedly slippery scramble between giant boulders to reach the road at the Meeting of the Three Waters.

We hitched a lift back to the hostel and in the evening over a pint at the nearby Clachaig Hotel we made plans to tackle more ambitious ascents the following day. These concerned the Aonagh Eagach Ridge on the opposite side of the glen, which was apparently one of the classic routes in Scottish mountaineering, particularly as a winter traverse. This was an ambitious project for our level of experience, but nothing ventured, nothing gained!

On the following day however, Torridon's rain seemed to have caught up with us, so we had to keep the venture on hold until the day after, which would be our last of the holiday. Meanwhile, rather than waste a wet day we walked right up to the other end of the glen, a distance of around eleven miles, as far as Kingshouse Hotel, where we ordered afternoon tea. We'd worked up such an appetite after our walk that we soon had all the scones and pancakes we'd been provided with polished off. Still feeling hungry we sneaked over to adjacent tables that had been vacated, and appropriated the scones that departing visitors had left behind. In fact we had rather too many eventually and didn't fully appreciate our dinner when we returned to the hostel!

On our last day the weather was fair so we set off for the far end of the Aonagh Eagach, with our intention being to walk back towards our base, where the ridge dropped down towards Clachaig Hotel. We had to hitch along to the starting point and a lorry driver obligingly stopped to pick us up. When we told him about our plans he squinted out the window and looked up at the ridge, before shaking his head in disbelief, muttering 'Bloomin mad'. We smirked, but a short while later we were beginning to think he might have a point!

It was tough, steep climbing up to the beginning of the ridge at Am Bodach, where we hit the snowline. The Chancellor was a short distance away and was extremely slippery, also the wind was escalating, providing a substantial chill factor. At the summit of the Chancellor we could see right along the ridge which looked decidedly intimidating at close quarters in its winter mantle and to get onto the next section of the ridge after the Chancellor involved negotiating a perpendicular drop covered in ice. Without crampons this was going to be tough and there was no saying what other nasty obstacles lay in store further along the narrow ridge, never mind the fact that once on it there was no escape until we reached the other end. I wanted to take my glove off to blow my nose, but as soon as I removed it my hand was sticking to the metal head of my axe. We dropped to our knees to peer over the edge of the forbidding drop and at this point Anne announced that one of her gloves had taken flight. We thought of the lorry driver's words and shuddered. We'd have to save up for crampons or try again in the summer. The deciding factor was when we remembered that the Dumbartonshire police were in the glen that week on a mountain rescue course – and we didn't fancy the indignity of having to be rescued by them if we got into difficulties, especially after having socialized with them in the pub the previous night!

Our last night in Glencoe was spent folk singing in Clachaig Hotel, as after that we had to return to college in Glasgow for our psychology exam, but the summer holidays were not too far away and we were planning Skye.

# 3

# A SOCIAL WHIRL IN SKYE

Our next expedition together was a week in Skye in the summer of 1963, following our graduation from college as primary school teachers. The prospect of now starting my career in the classroom was daunting. It didn't match my image, conjuring up visions of respectability, a smart two piece suit, saloon car, steady boyfriend, mortgaged semi and a package holiday on the Mediterranean! It wasn't for me. I was still trying to demolish the shackles of my strict Victorian childhood and at twenty-one I was not about to settle down.

Our week in Skye wasn't the most remarkable for climbing achievements, but on the other hand it was extremely notable for social exploits. It was late in the day when we left Pitlochry to hitchhike over to the west coast, prompting people we met on route to say, "You'll never reach Skye tonight!" Nevertheless we did, surprising even ourselves in the process. Being in the days before the Skye Bridge, we'd caught the last ferry of the day from Kyle of Lochalsh to Kyleakin and arrived on the island in darkness.

Anne had never been to Skye before and my only visit had been in 1958, shepherded by my parents and staying in Glen Brittle House Hotel. There was to be no luxury like that this time, as we would be camping in Anne's miniscule Andre Jamet. Our last lift dropped us in the vicinity of the hotel, which we could just make out in the darkness as we hoisted our packs onto the verge. I suggested camping a short distance up the valley at the back of the hotel where a footpath ran beside a convenient stream, so we plodded up to a suitable grassy hollow and erected the tent in the moonlight, with the faint ragged ridge of the Black Cuillins just visible high above.

In the morning the ridge was sharply etched against an azure sky, giving us a rush of adrenalin, and reminding me of how enthralled I'd been as a teenager when I'd first seen it. Anne was equally impressed, but there was dangerous stuff up there and we had no guide book. Previously I'd accessed the ridge via a climb called Window Buttress, which had been achieved in misty conditions with an experienced leader up front. Looking at the scene ahead of me now I didn't have the faintest idea of the whereabouts of Window Buttress. Instead we decided after consultation with our map to head for Coire Lagan where we could watch climbers on the nearby Cioch and the vertical walls of Sron na Ciche.

When we arrived there and found ourselves a pew amongst the rocks we saw several parties tackling what looked like desperate VS routes - VS signifying 'Very Severe' in mountaineering terminology. Such access to the summit of the ridge and its highest peak which was Sgurr Alasdair, was completely out of our league, leaving us with the only possibility being to climb up one of the famous scree shoots, usually reserved for skilled descents. After some hesitation we started ascending it and soon found that for every three steps up we slithered back down again for two. Only sheer determination and heavy breathing got us to the top where we found that to move right or left along the narrow and exposed ridge was not going to be easy. In fact we had gained it at one of the most difficult places and despite the exhilarating view in all directions we soon found we were stuck. To attempt anything too risky might be to make an exhibition of ourselves so we decided to retreat by the way we had come, relishing the speed with which we made the descent amidst the flying stones. Well that was fun - all that effort to reach the top undone in two minutes flat, bringing us back to where we'd started!

There were easier ways to reach the summit of Sgurr Alasdair but we had not yet sussed these out. We returned to our camp site and made tea, before deciding to walk along to the Glen Brittle Youth Hostel for some social chat and maybe some advice on routes to the various summits. My diary of the period was somewhat sketchy, so whether this achieved anything I'm not sure, because it was superseded by an unexpected shock when we returned to our tent in darkness. As we crawled inside with our torches the first thing they illuminated was a peremptory, scribbled message from the landlord of the glen, written on an empty strawberry pie packet. We were being informed that we had no business to be camping there and must move without delay to the official camp site on the shores of Loch Brittle!

We looked at each other in dismay, as Loch Brittle was about a mile away. I didn't even know there was an official camp site at that point. We considered hanging on until the morning, but that would waste half the next day and perhaps incur further wrath from the landlord, so reluctantly we began to throw stuff into our rucksacks and collapse the tent. There was a short cut to the shore behind the hotel but half way along it we found ourselves having to climb over a dry stone wall, topped with barbed wire fencing, which was quite an operation in the dark while loaded with gear. I lost my comb in the process as it fell out my pocket into long grass, then Anne announced she'd left her hair brush and the dixies behind. I wasted time looking for my comb with a torch while Anne said she'd be as well going back for her hair brush while I was rummaging. Why these vanity articles were so important I don't know! Possibly the female instinct to display to an attractive male climbing companion if one should conveniently appear!

By the time we reached the shore we felt like evicted crofters fleeing during the Clearances, but one bonus point in all this upheaval was that we noticed quite a number of tents lurking in the gloomy darkness of the site, so it might be worth while socially. It was well past midnight before we had our tent up again and retired to bed with a piece and cheese.

In the morning we realised that all our labours of the previous night to facilitate a full day's climbing had been wasted, because it was raining persistently. Climbing was ruled out so we hitched a lift into Portree to top up our provisions. As we walked up the glen a Jag stopped for us with leopard skin seats, a couple in front and two dogs in the back. We were glad to get a lift so quickly, but not so amused to find we soon had an energetic spaniel each, sitting in our laps, both of them soaking wet and their long silky hair covered in black grainy sand from the beach. They felt warm while ensconced, but once we alighted in Portree our trousers were cold, wet and filthy!

On our return journey we picked up a rattling van and the owner told us he was camping by Loch Brittle, not far from ourselves. His name was Mike. He talked incessantly and when we arrived at our destination he invited himself for tea in our tent! Had we done too well with the hair brush!? We tried to steer the conversation round to climbing, but he wasn't interested, like a few others on the site. We decided to be more circumspect in future with whom we fell in tow and agreed to share coffee. The communal tap had opportunities for meeting people as did the wash-up block, although the toilets left much to be desired and didn't encourage loitering.

There was an improvement in the weather the following day, but the ridge was well obscured in thick layers of mist, so once again there was no climbing. Instead the decision was made to go for a motor boat trip round to Loch Scavaig with Ronald Macdonald, the local postman, who was the owner of the boat. Half a dozen campers from the site also joined the queue for the excursion, including Mike and a climbing instructor from the youth hostel called Pete, who said it was his day off. At Loch Scavaig everyone disembarked for a sight-seeing scramble over the rocks towards Loch Coruisk, a dark hidden gem cradled in the arms of two subsidiary ridges of the Cuillins leading to the main ridge. On the return voyage from this adventure we dropped lines with hooks over the side of the boat at the mouth of Loch Brittle, and brought them up again within minutes, full of writhing mackerel. Pete, gutted the fish and sang folk songs, as an accumulation of gulls wheeled noisily overhead.

It was a grand sociable day out and when we returned to the camp site Anne invited everyone within earshot to a soiree in the evening at our tent, the smallest on the site of course. Eight of us managed to squash inside alongside ourselves - Ronald the boatman, Pete from the hostel, Mike, two Yorkshire butchers that Anne had met at the communal tap while collecting water for the soup, and another whose name and appearance I've forgotten. All were men – three each!

Our guests brought contributions for the party. Ronald's was a bottle of whisky, while ours was tea, coffee, biscuits, cheese and fruit cake. The craic was unbeatable, with Ronald expounding on the folklore of Skye, while Pete added endless tales of mountaineering escapades. The butchers' contribution was motor car scrapes and we brought out our epic tale of the year which concerned the Glen Coulin ghost in Torridon!

The party lasted until the dawn and only broke up when Pete said he'd have to get back to the youth hostel before he was reported missing.

Annoyingly the weather was brilliant in the morning, but Anne and I wasted half of it catching up on lost sleep in the tent. In the afternoon we were ashamed of ourselves for losing out on such a good climbing day. Instead we strolled on the beach and made up a programme of activities for the rest of the week, until we were waylaid by the Yorkshire butchers who invited us to go with them in the evening to a dance in Portree in the Skye Gathering Hall, with transport provided in their van. It looked like our Skye week was rapidly becoming more notable for its social events than its mountaineering accomplishments.

On day number five we had a plan to rectify our climbing inactivity. After all, one day out of four on the hills so far was nothing to be proud of, but a bit of carelessness first thing in the morning looked like scuppering that too. While we were making breakfast Anne tripped over the primus and burned her wrist, so we had to do some first aid. It was very painful initially, but after a short while she said we were going out whatever. The sun was blazing down under a cloudless sky when we left for the ridge at 12 noon, warding off biting clegs and other persistent insectivores. The heat made us feel like giving up as we gazed longingly at the cool waters of Loch Brittle far below, but we kept going and eventually reached the crest of the ridge near the summit of Sgurr Dearg, taking a different route to the one we'd followed before up the scree shoot. We arrived near the iconic Inaccessible Pinnacle, but refrained from attempting climbing on it, especially with Anne's burn injury. The views across the sea to the Outer Hebrides were stunning, with a thousand winking lights catching the crests of the waves. The rock scenery of the ridge corkscrewing like a monstrous black snake into the distance was spectacular too, while below us was the grey blue of the screes leading into verdant green grass and purple heather.

We managed to scramble round part of the ridge to Sgurr Banachdich before descending into Glen Brittle, chatting about the various men we had come into contact with during our vacation, most of whom had not turned out to be climbing companions despite their social attributes. The only serious climber was Pete who was tied up during the day with Youth Hostel course participants.

In the evening we were invited to a party at the hostel which was a rollicking affair with singing and yarn spinning that went on until the early hours of the morning and effectively put paid to our last full day on Skye as far as climbing was concerned. However, it was Friday and there was another dance to look forward to at night in the Skye Gathering Hall, with transport being provided once again by the Yorkshire butchers. At these events there was always a sharp division between the locals and the climber/camping fraternity of holiday incomers. We danced in our socks and trousers, while the local girls had layers of flared skirts, nylons and stilettos. The climbing girls were in short supply so one of the butchers had chatted up a local girl and was intent on seeing her home afterwards in his van. This of course was our transport back to Glen Brittle, but it had temporarily disappeared leaving three of us stranded in Portree Square with a long wait. The annoyance of this was compounded by the fact that a chill wind was blowing and we didn't have our warmest clothes on. With the continued absence of the van dragging on, Pete took matters into his own hands. He went round all the parked cars in the square trying the door handles until he found one that wasn't locked. He opened the rear door wide, shifted a string shopping bag from the back seat to the front, then ushered us all inside to shelter from the cold.

I was horrified. "We can't do this," I said in alarm. "It's not our car!"

"Well do you want to stand outside in the cold then? Who knows how long it will be before the van comes back for us?"

We groaned at this supposition, climbed aboard and sat down.

"What if the owner suddenly turns up?" I persisted

"He won't, not at 2 o'clock in the morning. These cars are parked overnight."

The owner didn't turn up but somebody else did – the police! They toured the square with search lights flashing, while consumed with guilt we ducked hastily behind the front seats, holding our breath. But the police car passed by without stopping and exited the square by the way it had come.

When our elusive driver eventually returned with the van we were ready to vent our wrath, but we kept some of it suppressed because the butchers had offered us a lift to Glasgow the following day.

It was 4am by the time we returned to the campsite. We didn't bother going to bed as the boys were anxious to get going on their long journey to Yorkshire. Packing up was done at once and our last view of the Cuillins as we rounded the corner at Sgurr nan Gillian was of the dawn mists rising from the hollows and the black ridge above bathed in a pinkish glow as the sunrise broke over the horizon.

# 4

# FlOODED OUT IN ARRAN

Our next notable holiday was in Arran, an island much further south than Skye, at the mouth of the Firth of Clyde and easily accessible from Glasgow. It was no less spectacular than some of the larger islands. In fact it had everything on a much smaller scale, including a range of imposing and rugged mountains in the north, with Goatfell, the highest of these, occupying a majestic position overlooking Brodick Bay. The more rugged mountains to the rear included the impressive A'Chir Ridge, a modest challenge for the intrepid hill walker. Glen Rosa gave access to this playground from Brodick and also provided a picturesque camping ground along the banks of the winding River Rosa, which was our destination as soon as we disembarked from the steamer at Brodick Pier.

We'd arrived on the island in the middle of an August heatwave and we had three miles to walk to the camping ground in sweltering heat, laden with gear. We struggled with our enormous packs and had numerous stops to relieve the weight and cool down, until our first view of the designated area lifted morale. Woodland shaded the Glen Rosa track on our left, and to the right, meadows of sun scorched grass sloped downhill to the bends in the river. It was an unofficial camp site with no tap, toilets, waste disposal, shop, in fact nothing at all, except the rather depleted sparkling water of the River Rosa below high sandy embankments. We pitched our tent in the crook of one of the bends, handy for water supplies, and having completed the task we relaxed on the embankment in our shorts and T-shirts, squinting up at the view through the tinted glass of our shades. The mountains appeared hazy with distance, but there were a few stalwart walkers on the glen track, while campers in the meadow pottered listlessly, or sat on the embankments lazily trailing their feet in the cool waters of the river.

Other occupants of the area were sheep, most of whom were crouching in hollows below banks of thirsty heather, but at night when the temperature dropped they came into their own and made a great deal of troublesome bleating noise when we were trying to sleep, effectively keeping us awake for hours.

In the morning the sun was blazing down again and bringing to life the less attractive forms of insect life. However, we had plans for an ascent of Goatfell on our first day, so we gathered necessary equipment and set off up the dry, sandy track which was blistered with days of intense heat, patterned with cracks from grilling under the relentless sun and bordered with yellow scorched grass. Glen Rosa was also a favourite haunt of adders and they all seemed to be on a day out as we marched along, basking in the dry sandy hollows, or baking on a smooth slab of rock nearby. Fortunately there was no chance of them spitting at us in the passing, as they were all far too sleepily content for that. In addition to the reptile life underfoot there were myriads of coloured butterflies enjoying their short life in the sun, interspersed with unwelcome clegs ready to attack exposed arms and legs.

We reflected on the weather for climbing which was far from ideal. That was the problem with mountaineering – often ranging from too hot, wet, misty, gale force winds, icy or too perishing cold. The days when it was just right were few and far between. One just had to make the best of things and treat it as part of the adventure.

Climbing uphill in the intense heat was a struggle and by the time we reached the saddle at the top of Glen Rosa we were bathed in sweat! There was still a long way to go from the saddle to attain the summit of Goatfell at 2,866 feet and continuing at that particular point was unthinkable. Instead we plunged into the river and climbed onto a large smooth slab mid-stream, partly shaded by a rowan tree. There we stretched out in the sun, trailing our hot, sticky hands in the ice cold water below.

Occasionally we looked up at our objective which looked an interesting scramble, so with an effort we eventually roused ourselves and set off for the skyline. A cooling breeze encouraged us as we gained height amongst the rocks, heather and coarse tussock grass and we made rapid progress towards the summit. An amazing view greeted us as we looked over the other side towards Brodick Bay and the Holy Isle, but there was also an unattractive collection of discarded litter near the cairn, left behind by hoards of tourists who ascended the mountain by the tourist path from Brodick! We had earmarked this path for our descent, but it was a very long meandering trail.

We made a beeline for the nearest ice cream shop after arriving in Brodick and ordered Knickerbocker Glories. They were so refreshing that we felt like purchasing another but the café was closing. Instead Anne suggested fish and chips and joined a lengthy queue behind a smoking 'fried supper' bus in the square. So much for bringing all our provisions from Glasgow!

The following day there was no let-up in the heatwave, although a few patches of mist were creeping in. We slept late and decided to have a rest day before attempting the ridge on the other side of the glen. In the afternoon however, we decided to walk down to Brodick to eye up the talent and summer attractions. The main activity seemed to be water skiing in the bay, where a bill board on the shore advertised a trip round the bay for seven shillings and six pence (37 pence and a half penny in new money), or three falls. It was inviting, but as we watched other tourists having a go, most of them seemed to have three falls and some of them never got onto the surface of the water at all. We began to reconsider whether it was worth it to try on a pair of water skis and topple head first three times into a patch of petrol stained water, because there was obviously an art to it that had to be learned over a period of time! We got up from the bench we'd been sitting on and went back across the road to the knickerbocker café instead and played crazy golf in the garden adjoining it.

On returning to the campsite we started preparations for our evening meal and seeing two fellows erecting a tent nearby we hatched a plan to borrow some salt as a means of making social contact. We got the salt, but further contact at the time wasn't very extensive! As it was Saturday night we decided to walk into Brodick in the evening for drinks at the Ormidale Hotel. In those days we thought nothing of the three mile walk each way and the fact that we would have notched up twelve miles during the day without climbing a mountain was not considered a chore.

The evening's entertainment in Brodick proved to be better than expected with rousing folk singing at the Ormidale. The bar closed at 10pm as was the custom in the sixties, and afterwards the assembled company repaired to the local dance hall across the road. Here we secured the attention of the two chaps from the campsite who had been the recipients of our salt borrowing campaign earlier and after a boisterous old time dancing session the boys offered us a lift home to the campsite.

"Fantastic!" we cheered, thinking of the three mile walk back to the campsite in the dark with distaste. But when we arrived in the gravel forecourt outside the hall and discovered that the transport was to be push bikes we were somewhat deflated. Hired bicycles were commonplace in Arran. Many garages supplied them and they came in particularly handy for campers and hostellers to access accommodation.

"You two can sit on the saddles," the boys chuckled. "We'll pedal."

Well there was nothing like surprises in Arran. We jumped on and grabbed the waist in front as the lusty peddlers, having consumed rather too much drink, swung out of the forecourt. It was a peg better than walking, but I couldn't help thinking it was going to be a precarious expedition. Without the customary foot support it was difficult to maintain balance and to make things more awkward my peddling partner had a guitar slung over his shoulder - and dangling over the handlebars was a string bag and a pair of basketball boots tied by the laces. After leaving the outskirts of the village behind we became aware of another serious inconvenience. The bicycles had no lights and it was pitch dark. Undeterred by this disadvantage my partner continued on his way, sweating and puffing up a steep hill with great determination, wobbling and swaying in low gear, until at last he let out a sigh of satisfaction, "Phew - we made it," he gasped.

I breathed a sigh of relief but all was not yet over. Having arrived at the top of the hill the machine suddenly gathered speed as we zoomed down the other side in Stygian darkness. There was no sight or sound of the others as we rocketed on, sometimes on the grass verge and sometimes on the gravel at the side of the road. I hung on tight to the gyrating hips in front as I peered into the inky blackness and shouted that we were going far too fast for the conditions – but it was too late - we'd left tar macadam behind and were jolting over rough ground, stones and clumps of vegetation. Then unexpectedly the machine forcibly upended itself and we were thrown into a dense cluster of rhododendron bushes!

"Sorry!" he apologised as we staggered out of the undergrowth brushing ourselves down and sincerely grateful for the soft landing. I refused to remount, so we walked the rest of the way to the campsite. Anne arrived twenty minutes later saying she had dismounted about a mile out of Brodick after the saddle slipped back.

Our plans for the following day were to tackle the A'Chir Ridge, but as soon as we pulled back the tent flaps in the morning we realised with dismay that the heatwave had ended and rain was descending. The sky looked ominous too, with low grey cloud cover. There was an oppressive feel to the atmosphere as if something unpleasant was brewing. Perhaps we were in for a thunderstorm?

Initially the rain was light, but persistent. Other campers in the meadow were packing up, including our push biking partners, but we decided to sit tight for another day to see if there was an improvement. After all there were still things we wanted to achieve in the area. Too many of our mountaineering holidays had led to under achievement in the hills – so this was not going to be one of them.

The off and on rain situation continued all day and led to inactivity, but in the evening we decided to liven things up with a five mile walk to the far side of Brodick, where we'd heard there was a dance on at a venue called 'The Shieling', due to start at 1am on Monday morning. The reason behind this absurd starting time was to avoid clashing with religious activities on the Sabbath and upsetting the local population! We thought it would be a novelty to attend a dance that started after midnight, but the occasion did not quite match up to expectations. It was well attended by young people all intent on brightening up an extremely dull Sunday, but there was no vibrant buzz. Long hair was becoming fashionable for men and it was sometimes difficult to distinguish between male and female, except that the men's hair in this category seemed to be particularly greasy as they had perhaps not yet cottoned on to the fact that long hair took time and patience to manage! We spent most of the night saying to each other, "Would you look at that?"

Eventually in the absence of no fanciable men and more rain pending, we decided to head back to the campsite, and when we arrived we noticed through the gloom that there were very few tents remaining. Without looking about too much we unzipped the tent opening, crawled into our sleeping bags and fell asleep almost immediately.

As we slept the rain escalated and when we wakened in the morning we were aware of drips descending from the canvas roof. Worse than that we were aware that the river was roaring nearby, accompanied by the wind howling through the forest above the Glen Rosa track. It didn't encourage us to go outside, or to light the primus for breakfast. We made do with bread and honey and digestive biscuits and we traced the drips on the tent roof down to the groundsheet with our fingers, which was a trick some campers employed in wet weather to keep rain from falling onto clothes and sleeping bags.

During the morning we made a quick dive outside to spend a penny behind the tent, and when we had a brief look around things were not looking good. Sheets of rain were sweeping across the waterlogged and desolate site, where there was no sign of any other remaining tents and above us the sky was black and angry looking. However, we were stalwarts for hanging on and hoping that the weather would improve.

We decided to brave it out and with the decision made we retreated into the driest corner of our Lilliputian home and began singing through all the folk songs in our notebooks.

By mid afternoon the dry corner of the tent was wet and there were puddles on the groundsheet. We bundled most things into our rucksacks and sat on the floor in our shorts between the puddles. If we could last the night it was sure to be better tomorrow was our resolve, but we'd have to scrape up something for dinner. Anne grabbed a dixie and went outside to get water for a cup of tea to get us in the mood. I heard her paddling about in the long soaking grass outside, then a blood curdling scream that made me drop the dishes I was holding and dive outside the tent to see what had happened.

Too much - it transpired! The river had risen dramatically and burst its banks - that's what. We had camped in the crook of a wide river bend and the meanders on either side of us had caved in sending the river rushing and whooshing across the gap. We were marooned on an island with raging torrents trapping us in a marshy sea of devastation all around. Without wasting a minute we dived into the tent, stuffed our remaining possessions into the packs, collapsed the soaking tent, hauled up the pegs, and bundling the sodden canvas between us we looked about for an exit. The only thing we could do was head for the area where the river was flooding across the gap which might be less deep, in the hope that we could still wade and climb the meadow on the other side to the Glen Rosa track. We had no other choice as to stay put was unthinkable.

When we reached the edge of the new water channel we plunged in with our sandshoes on. The muddy water was churning and boiling in strong gurgling waves, and it was full of ripped up vegetation and torn branches of trees. We hung on grimly to our possessions as the water crept up to our knees and tugged at our thighs. The swirling, rushing current threatened to unbalance us, but we ploughed on and at last the water receded as we staggered out the far side and paddled through marshy hollows to reach the track above. When we looked back at the turmoil we'd left behind in the flooded valley we were stunned and horrified at our narrow escape. We'd been too complacent with the heat wave weather, not expecting it to break and we'd had no means of communication to keep up with the daily weather forecasts.

It was a lesson learned in mountain craft and we'd been lucky to have got away with such impending disaster. "Well," said Anne, "At least we have the distinction of being the last to leave the site." We'd been well and truly last and a trifle irresponsible into the bargain. Now we had to decide what to do. We couldn't walk to the youth hostel trailing our bundles of soggy gear and we hadn't enough money for a bed and breakfast, even supposing anyone would let us in the door in our mud streaked and dishevelled state. There was only one option left, which was to hurry as quickly as we could to the pier and see if there was still a boat leaving for the mainland that night. We were lucky in this respect and caught the last steamer of the day with two minutes to spare. It took us to Fairlie, instead of Ardrossan, but we managed to get a train from there straight into Glasgow.

It was a right anti-climax arriving in Glasgow Central Station, like two tramps from the wilderness, just having survived a major disaster. But the main thing was – we were survivors! What next was going to try us?

It was a freezing camp at New Year 1965, with streams full of ice in the wilds of Glen Nevis.

# 5

## FROZEN IN GLEN NEVIS

Amongst our various mountaineering holidays in the Highlands and Islands we had not yet experienced one at New Year, but this was going to be our next venture. Anne had told me that Glasgow Clubs and Mountain Rescue organisations congregated in Glen Nevis at New Year for a long weekend of riotous celebrations and she suggested we take a tent along and join them. Mountaineering was not much mentioned in connection with it, but I had a suspicion that alcohol figured prominently. Not being much of a social drinker this was one thing that bothered me about the expedition. I didn't like whisky of any description, including malt which was the National drink for these occasions and I only drank beer drowned in lemonade. Bacardi was OK with a dash of coke, but it wasn't everyone's tipple, especially at New Year. All things considered and nips being out of the question I felt I wouldn't score very highly on the popularity scale with Glasgow male climbers, never mind anybody else. However, I agreed to go. It was an opportunity too good to miss at the foot of Scotland's highest mountain and it could hardly be worse than the floods we'd had to battle with in Arran, or the supernatural peculiarities of Torridon.

I met Anne in Glasgow and spent the night at her house as we were leaving at half past four on hogmanay morning to catch a train to Fort William. We'd decided we had too much baggage to hitch as Anne had borrowed a much larger tent for this weekend, an Arctic Guinea, and since we would be camping in January we'd taken extra clothes and newspapers for insulation under the sleeping bags. I had not camped out at New Year before which was going to be another novel experience.

We had all the gear, clothes and food divided between three rucksacks and as there was a three mile walk up Glen Nevis to the designated camping spot, we decided to leave one rucksack in the left luggage office at Fort William station when we arrived. The attendant at the counter was well impressed when he heaved our pack into the back office, this one being the heaviest of the three - the contents of which we intended to split between two packs when we returned.

During our walk up the glen I shivered in the cold, frosty weather. The camping spot just beyond the youth hostel was white with a dusting of snow, covering iron-hard frozen ground below and the river nearby, which we were depending on for water for the tea was glistening with ice. Anne was expecting two female friends to join us, who were students from Glasgow University, but so far they had not arrived. She also told me about the Langside Club members who arrived by private bus from Glasgow, generally after midnight on Hogmanay and camped just up the glen from where we were situated. She seemed to know quite a few of them and mentioned that a guy nicknamed Jigsaw would be an excellent match for me. "What do you mean by that?" I asked, thinking – 'Is this a pairing off exercise?' I didn't want to be manipulated as I already had a boyfriend in Pitlochry although he was shortly going to sea to join the catering staff on a cruise liner sailing to Australia - not a good omen for continuation of the relationship!

Our return to Fort William to fetch the third rucksack from the station notched up nine miles of walking that day and having risen at 4 o'clock in the morning I was starting to flag. After picking up our final pack and splitting the contents between two we went to a local supermarket to get booze supplies. Anne agreed to the purchase of a bottle of Bacardi and half a dozen bottles of coke and lemonade and we joined an enormous queue to pay for them. When we arrived at the check out however an unexpected barney ensued with the girl at the cash desk when I asked for paper bags to separate the bottles. "D'you think I've time on Hogmanay to put bottles in bags?" she exploded.

"Just give me the bags and I'll do it." I said bristling, after which I received a heated resume of all the things she had to do and the people she had to attend to before closing time! Meanwhile Anne was making for the door in embarrassment, so I swept up the bottles, three in each hand with much noisy clinking, and in the street outside we stuffed them into the rucksacks, along with the Bacardi. As we marched back up the road to the tent I couldn't help wondering where the New Year spirit was, because it didn't seem to be much evident in the shops of Fort William!

Anne's friends had arrived when we returned so we all cooked dinner, after which it was decided we were returning to town for a round of the pubs – despite another three mile walk to get there. After a quick circuit we settled on the Imperial as being the leader for entertainment, with rousing folk singing to the twang of guitars, so we squeezed onto a table end and ordered drinks. As the night wore on the crowd and the volume of noise increased until it was almost impossible to get to the bar counter to place further orders, far less get back to our corner without spilling them. By closing time the singing was being conducted from numerous table tops by inebriated individuals whose batons were pint glasses and carry out bags!

Some well intoxicated lad from the Fleet Air Arms had meanwhile fastened himself to Anne and insisted on accompanying us back up the glen, until he realised how far we were going and promptly disappeared. At midnight the four of us brought in the New Year in our tent with rum-laced tea and a slice of fruit gingerbread, before looking around for something more exciting to do. The intention had been to go up to the Langside camp and first foot them, but they had still not arrived from Glasgow, presumably having a bevy in every pub along the way.

We stood outside our tents in the frosty night, which was surprisingly clear, with a thousand stars winking overhead and a pale glow from the moon illuminating the faint outline of Ben Nevis high above the glen. There wasn't a sound below. So much for tales of all the New Year hilarity in the glen. It certainly wasn't here. We didn't feel like turning in either as it was far too perishing cold to sleep. "We could go up to Polldubh," it was voiced suddenly. "The navy boys will be there from Lossiemouth."

Polldubh was a cottage two and a half miles further up the glen, which was used by the navy for training exercises in the area. Despite the extra walking it would keep us warm so we collected some bottles into a rucksack and with one torch between us we set off at 1am. After our evening's dramming at the Imperial we fairly danced up the road, spinning yarns along the way, but when we arrived at the cottage we found that the occupants had gone to bed.

"I'll soon get them up," said Anne and she went careering through their dormitory clinking bottles and hooting like a Red Indian! The fellows we discovered were all English and seemed to be unaware of the extensive celebrations that went on in the Highlands to bring in the New Year. The sight of four cavorting high spirited females soon roused them however and we gathered round their kitchen table, found an assortment of cups and poured drams. The night wore on and as our stamina waned so did some of the jokes and hilarity. I yawned uncontrollably and missed the point in most of the wisecracks through not paying attention, so I was glad when the decision was made to head off.

It seemed a very long trudge back to the campsite in a stiff breeze and sleety rain which kept us awake, but soaked us to the skin. After all we had now been up for twenty-four hours and clocked up a total of twenty-three miles walking on the glen road. In the passing we noticed that the Langside tents had arrived, but they were in darkness and it was half past four in the morning, so we kept on walking until we reached our own tents and crawled into our sleeping bags. We shivered with the cold despite being desperate to sleep and I couldn't help thinking that none of the fellows at Polldubh had really been worth the five mile round trip we'd made to visit them! I couldn't see much climbing being done over this holiday and the other three had never mentioned the subject. I was becoming completely disillusioned, because climbing had always come first for me in front of social life. And what social life was there anyway in the freezing glen? If tonight was anything to go by I'd have had a better New Year in Pitlochry, sitting round cheery log fires, drinking punch, eating Christmas cake, shortbread and the customary Black Bun.

Despite these perverse thoughts a new day and a new year was dawning, although the first half of it was spent recovering from the day before. We made breakfast at lunch time, then later in the afternoon we took a wander down towards the youth hostel and Cameron's Barn, where the Kinloss Mountain Rescue Team were spending the weekend. We had not so far seen any sign of them, but as we passed by a few of their members were standing outside. We fell into conversation with them and two minutes later we were inside the barn, sitting on a bale of hay, dram in hand and a welcome blow heater in front of us that the boys called 'The Bomb'. We were really glad of its heat which encouraged us to linger as long as possible and join in with a folk singing session in progress.

The sleeping accommodation for the men was in the hayloft above, reached by a ladder and they were using the pigsty downstairs for their kitchen, fortunately minus pig. The atmosphere was laden with the odour of farm stock, dung and damp clothes, but the generous supply of heat made us hang on. When the team announced that they were going to a dance in Kinlochleven in the evening and invited us to accompany them in the Mountain Rescue truck we readily agreed. Anything was better than another night in the Arctic Guinea which was living up to its name.

I was used to appearing at village dances in climbing areas in my mountaineering garb, but this was to be my debut in wellington boots! Nor was I ever short of dancing partners when we arrived, probably due to the preponderance of men! Back in the glen afterwards it was another glorious frosty night, with the moon casting its light across the snows of the Ben. I wished I was standing on the skyline instead of down in the valley where it was perishing cold. The ground below our feet was iron hard with puddles transformed into skeletal sheets of dry and brittle steel, while the grass was like spears of glittering white and the river was silent beneath its ice encrusted mantle.

We loitered outside the tents trying to invent excuses for not turning in, as sleep in such sub zero temperatures would be impossible. Then we heard a shout and saw a lone figure approaching us from the direction of the Langside camp. It turned out to be Ronnie, the leader of the Training Centre, more generally referred to as a club. He said he wanted to borrow soap, which we thought was a paltry excuse for visiting us girls. Anne knew him and invited him into our tent for a dram. He could talk for Scotland and spent what was left of the night spinning all the crazy yarns and ghost stories at his command. After he left sleep was still unthinkable on the freezing ground, despite wearing all our clothes inside our sleeping bags, and our layer of newspapers supposed to be protecting us against the frost below. I even had my gloves and balaclava on, but I only dozed for ten minute snatches before wakening again, chittering with cold. During the short periods I slept I dreamed of a blazing fire, a hot, steamy bath and the aroma of sizzling, roast chicken, only to be completely disillusioned on waking to find myself still immersed in unpleasant Arctic weather.

I didn't consider the holiday so far to have been much of a success and if I had been hoping to strike up a new relationship with someone, a Don Juan of the climbing world, then I didn't think there would be much chance of that either in my present untidy, unwashed and exhausted state. The intention had been to stay until the following day, but I didn't think I could last that long without a decent sleep. No – I was going today, as soon as I could get packed up and on the road hitchhiking. I leaned over to tell Anne of my intentions, but she wasn't there. Well that put the tin hat on it. She had gone off somewhere without telling me? I suspected she might be at the Langside camp looking up an old boyfriend she had talked about - not that the assumption bothered me, but the Arctic cold did and the lack of warm insulated clothing, coupled with lack of sleep, which was leading to irrational and negative thoughts. I was getting the hell out of this unwelcome refrigerator at the first possible minute, but even as I started to drag my pack out the tent a thread of reason returned telling me – 'You can't just disappear. Go to the Langside camp first and tell Anne you're leaving.'

I left my pack where it was and ran across the frozen turf until I got to the camp. I saw their large bell tent amongst a cluster of smaller ones so I stuck my head in the door and asked if anyone had seen Anne. The answer was 'no' and she had not been there either, but Ronnie suddenly rose from his seat beside their calor gas cooker and beckoned me to come in. I was about to refuse and say that I was leaving, then on a last minute whim I said, "By the way – who's Jigsaw?" I might as well have a quick look at what kind of a fellow Anne had decided would be so suitable for me!

Ronnie followed the remark immediately by shouting, "Hey James! Here's one of your admirers!" while I stood there totally embarrassed and trying to think up some plausible excuse for having mentioned his name. Meanwhile an expectant head shot out of a rucksack he was packing climbing gear into and looked in my direction.

"I'm sorry, I'm just going," I said, while Ronnie waved a warm bacon sandwich towards me along with an invitation to take a seat and join their company. The sandwich looked inviting and there was a fair heat coming from their stove. One part of me wanted to repeat, "I can't stay." But another part of me hesitated. Then Jigsaw spoke, "Hey, you don't have to race off. I'm going climbing with my mate, but stay at the tent and get warm and join us in the evening. We're all going to the pub in the Fort and we're having a party in the bell tent after. You're very welcome."

I hesitated again, but I sat down on a lilo and ate my sandwich and drank a steaming mug of tea. Maybe I could just stay one more night - and Jigsaw I thought was definitely worth getting to know, as I tried not to let him see me watching him leave, a rope neatly coiled on his back and the flash of silver steel on his axe. I should be out there too, not sitting here moaning about the cold. I noticed the more experienced climbers all had Duvet jackets for winter relaxation. It was the latest thing for keeping warm as well as a good Icelandic Special sleeping bag and a lilo mattress underneath. I would have to save up and buy the proper stuff.

As I warmed up morale lifted. Ronnie and I and a few others who remained at the camp had great craic, before I returned to our tent to unpack my rucksack.

"Where've you been?" Anne asked as I pulled back the tent flap.

"Up at the Langside camp looking for you," I replied. "When I wakened this morning you weren't here! Where were you?"

She said she'd been down in the Fort looking for Askit Powders and hadn't wanted to waken me. Then she asked why my stuff was packed. "Well actually," I said, "I'd been considering leaving."

"Don't be daft," she replied quickly. "Hang on until tomorrow and we'll all go together."

"That's what I'm going to do," I said and without further explanation I unpacked my gear.

It was early evening when Anne and I and the girls set off once again for the town, making for the Imperial to get a decent wash with hot water in the ladies cloakroom, before meeting up with the Langside. Dwindling finances led to us ordering tomato juice in the bar and we were consuming these when Ronnie appeared round the door shouting across to us, "What are you lassies doing in here? I've come to escort you to the Jacobite."

It was a short walk back along the Main Street to reach the designated place and once installed there I soon found myself sharing a bench with Jigsaw. We talked climbing and sang until closing time, when a large carryout was purchased for the party in the bell tent. As we made our way towards the glen road however there was a major calamity. One of the Langsiders dropped a full bottle of whisky in the middle of the main road. There were stricken howls of despair and anger while the party gathered round the spilled remains, giving them the last rights as it were and completely blocking the road to traffic, although the recumbent circle quickly dispersed on the appearance of the local police patrol. The culprit was then chased up the glen, while Jigsaw and I managed to secure a lift in a mini and arrived back at camp before most of the others.

We stood outside for a while admiring the view in the moonlight, and the horseshoe of splendid glittering peaks at the head of the glen.

He was now aware that I came from Perthshire and that I was obsessed with mountains, so he made me a sudden unexpected offer. "Been abroad before? Would you like to go to the Dolomite Alps in Italy this summer with the club? We go there every other year to climb on the Dolomite towers, but this time some of the girls wanted to go as well and do high level walking between the huts. Three of them are going, but it would be better to have four. Would you like to make up the number?"

I was speechless, before replying, "Definitely! That would be fantastic. I've never been to the continent."

Almost before I could get over this amazing offer he was rambling on again with another proposition. "If you really want to get into major climbing you should come and live in Glasgow where you can join the Langside and come to Glencoe with us at weekends. You'll find most climbers in the cities, not in the country."

I thought about what he'd said. It made sense. I was at a crossroads in my life, being nearly finished my two years of probationary teaching practice in Perthshire and having fallen out with my parents on numerous occasions over my scruffy mountaineering companions and my non-adherence to the Victorian ideal. I had to get away, but I had the vaguest idea where. Jigsaw had just thrown me a lifeline and I grabbed it with two hands. My life would never be the same again.

As for the party in the bell tent – it was hilarious. Despite the draughty seats and the cold wind filtering in beneath the canvas - the craic, the singing, the atmosphere and the fried burger rolls were superb. I was no longer at a loose end. Thanks to Jigsaw and Anne I knew where I was going.

# PART 2: THE DOLOMITES 1965

# 1

# TRAINING ON THE WEST COAST

After two years with Anne I was now moving on to new hill walking companions. Life was about moving on – from Glenmore Lodge in the Cairngorms to exploits in the Western Highlands and now to the Dolomites in Italy. I was progressing to more advanced stuff - higher peaks - longer treks - and possibly heavier pack carrying, though some of the stuff Anne and I carried would be hard to beat!

Jigsaw kept in touch with travel details to Italy and I was invited to attend a weekend in Glasgow, when slides were being shown of previous Dolomite trips held by the Langside. This was a marathon presentation of the general terrain, revealing perpendicular pinnacles devoid of vegetation and daunting rock routes which I hoped were only intended for the men. I was both awestruck and intimidated, but I was assured that the girls would mainly be walking over the high passes between the towers with the option of tackling 'via ferrata' routes to spice things up. ('via ferratas' being exposed rock routes with fixed ropes, steel ladders and pitons screwed to the rock for use as footholds.)

The girls' group was being organised by Susan who had been at Jordanhill around the same time as I had, although I'd never met her. The other two girls were teenagers, Jane and Susie, who had recently left school and were waiting to go to University. I was twenty-three and they were eighteen, but I've kept in touch with Jane for over fifty years, such is the bond you acquire with shared enthusiasm for mountaineering and the outdoors.

Susan and I being older, were deemed to be in charge and in this respect she invited me to spend a weekend with her in Glasgow so that we could become acquainted and plan our route between mountain huts in the area. The Dolomites, being part of the European Alpine chain were at the eastern end of it, but their geological composition and appearance was different. They were composed of rough limestone, abundant in holds and they were characterized by sheer, vertical, soaring spires, or larger blocks with expansive bald faces. The texture of the rock made them popular with climbers, although the exposure more than made up for this on the spine chilling scale - and being lower than the Swiss and French Alps they also held onto less snow. Scots climbers referred to the Dolomites as 'The Dollies' which I found quite amusing.

Susan had all the relevant maps of the area so we worked out a schedule between huts, taking in several of the major regions. We also planned a training session in Scotland at the beginning of July as a warm up to long distance trekking with packs and including a traverse of the Aonach Eagach Ridge in Glencoe to get used to exposure. I was pleased about the latter, seeing it as a chance for redemption against previous failure!

It was the 4th of July when Susan, Jane and I left to hitch north to Fort William, Susie not being able to join us due to a previous engagement. Three was not a good number for hitching, but if we split into two and one it left someone on their own. We decided to stick together and watched dismally as private cars with only room for two passed by, but we got lucky when an open backed lorry stopped and conveyed us to Crianlarich, where we had another tedious wait before swapping the discomforts of the lorry for something considerably worse - a packed Land Rover with three RAF canoeists bound for Fort William. The three men were sitting in the front and the back was almost totally occupied with gear, apart from a space of about twelve inches between the luggage and the roof. We were invited to lie out side by side in this restricted space, with our chins pressed against the back of the front seats and our feet jammed against the rear window. There was hardly room to wriggle more than a few inches and during the seventy mile journey Susan had to ask them to stop twice to relieve cramp. The men were good company and apologised for the abysmal accommodation, but as it was a lift directly to the door of our overnight lodgings at Glen Nevis Youth Hostel it was not to be sniffed at, so we waved inconveniences aside. On arriving at our destination we discovered another motive for their generosity. They were three men and we were three lassies and before their departure we found we had a pressing invitation to join them again in the evening for fish suppers and craic in Fort William! We decided we'd be able to handle the situation and accepted!

The following day we left from the Youth Hostel for our marathon seventeen mile trek through Glen Nevis and Steall Gorge on route to Loch Ossian Youth Hostel. After negotiating the boulder strewn path through the gorge with the Water of Nevis thundering through a narrow channel of jumbled rock beside us, the terrain widened as we passed by Steall Waterfall and saw the hut owned by the Lochaber Mountaineering Club on the other side of the river. It was accessed by a wire bridge of rather precarious proportions, which encouraged us to stop and have a go at crossing it, before beginning the long wilderness tramp south through the Mamore Mountains. On the way to Loch Treig we passed two more bothies, Luibeilt and Staoineag and at the second of these we stopped for a break. Some lads were sitting on the grass outside brewing tea and they offered us a cup so we hung around, glad to drop off our packs and relax. The boys were Royal Navy recruits from Lossiemouth, also on an exercise and when they heard how far we had walked and that we still had six miles to complete our trip, their officer in charge promptly mustered a couple of his men to join him and carry our packs to Loch Ossian. This wasn't really the object of our exercise and it felt a bit like cheating, but we let them do it nevertheless! I wondered what they might expect in return, but fortunately there was safety in numbers when we reached the hostel and after a few cups of coffee they left.

The hostel was one of the most remote and basic in Scotland, being eleven miles from the nearest motor road at Rannoch, although it could be reached by train from Corrour Station, just one mile distant. The building which was only used in the summer had no electricity or running water. At night the common room was lit by a tilly lamp that hissed, flickered and spluttered, sending bizarre shadows around the room - and water was fetched in a pail from nearby Loch Ossian. The warden was a student who sat in the corner of the common room in the evening, reading a book by the light of the lamp.

Shortly after we'd prepared and eaten dinner Jane and Susan retired to the dormitory, but I stayed up to write my diary and chat to the warden who was not at all bad looking in the lamplight! In the morning however, he looked different!

After breakfast and our cleaning jobs at the hostel which was the custom in the 1960's, we walked to Corrour Station and caught a train across the Rannoch Moor to Tulloch in Glen Spean. We had a free ride as no one came round and asked for any fares! At Tulloch we hitched a lift through Fort William and on to Glencoe Youth Hostel where we booked in for the next two nights.

The following day was to be our traverse of the Aonach Eagach Ridge from west to east, starting at Clachaig Hotel and ascending a steep footpath towards Sgor nam Fionnaidh high above Clachaig Gully. Brilliant sunshine accompanied our traverse and it was exhilarating to romp along the high narrow ridge, climbing over various tops and rock pinnacles along the way. Of course it was a different proposition in the summer to being encased in winter ice and snow when Anne and I had been stumped at the Chancellor. The views were totally amazing, the exposure thrilling and I was well satisfied at having overcome previous shortcomings to complete this classic traverse at last.

In the evening we celebrated our achievements with drinks at Clachaig Hotel, where a guitarist was entertaining and as some of his songs were new to me I begged a sheet of paper from the barman to write down the words.

Next morning we headed back south as there was only a week to go before we left for Italy and the Dolomites. I could hardly wait. In the middle of that week I had to attend the wedding of an old school and college friend from Perthshire. I thought to myself, 'How boring to be getting married. I'd rather be free, roaming in the mountains.' Then I remembered what someone had once said about me at college during a discussion on marriage and boyfriends. 'Liz will never get married, because she's married already. She's married to the mountains!' Surprisingly I didn't take offence at the remark. I was actually chuffed that they realised mountaineering figured as my chief interest!

# 2

# BOLZANO AND SASSOLUNGA

Members of the Langside booked on the Dolomite holiday met at Victoria Station in London on Saturday morning 17th July, but it was not until we arrived in Ostend and boarded our first trans-continental train for the fourteen hour journey to Munich in Bavaria that I had a surge of excitement at imminently seeing the Alps – or so I thought! Belgium of course was flat, interspersed with multi coloured brick houses and a patchwork quilt of agricultural land with no elevations to be seen on the horizon. We travelled swiftly across the endless plains under a dull grey sky, and with nothing particular to see out the window I turned my attention to what was happening in our compartment, this being a mixture of card games and chess. Then I noticed a change – not altogether pleasant. A strong smell of something disagreeable had pervaded the compartment. All eyes turned to the window which was open and the culprit was immediately identified as dung, which had been liberally spread across the nearby fields. The window was slammed shut despite the stifling heat within and in the general upheaval the chess pieces landed on the floor and the bishop was lost under the seat. Despite much crawling around and poking underneath with an ice axe shaft it didn't come to light, so attention was switched to food, making up ham rolls and pieces with jam. A short while later, rain was pelting down outside and running down the window panes in dirty diagonal streaks.

I gave up looking for the Alps and felt slightly disillusioned with the whole experience as the day wore on and it grew dark outside, shutting down the passing scene. The seats were narrow and hard and our carriage was divided into separate compartments with a corridor down one side. Ahead of us was a whole night of sitting, but we tried to sleep with our feet stretched across packs on the floor, but it was almost impossible with people clattering up and down the corridor outside conversing in foreign languages, officials demanding to see tickets and passports and stops at intervening stations with all the noise and mayhem that involved – clattering trolleys rumbling along the platform – luggage thumping - doors slamming – scurrying footsteps – shouting – whistles blowing – squeaking and clanking underneath the carriage! The seating meanwhile was not conducive to napping, but it was excellent for cultivating a stiff neck!

We arrived in Munich at 6am extremely relieved to see the back of our overnight conveyance and found we had an hour to wait for the connection that would take us through the Brenner Pass in Austria and on to our final destination at Bolzano in North Italy. Again I searched the landscape for a sign of the Alps, but there was still nothing visible through the grey misty dawn that hung around the buildings in the vicinity of Munich Station. Susan was chuffed though, because she got a packet of cigarettes from a machine on the station platform for a British half penny! This had all the boys turning out their pockets for similar coins.

Our train for Bolzano left at 7am and was considerably upmarket with well upholstered seats that could be converted into couchettes by sliding the seat forward with a leather strap. We took advantage of this and soon most of us were snoring despite a few interruptions from passport and customs officials.

Not long after crossing into Austria we heard a loud cheer from the corridor, the compartment door crashed open and one of our lads who'd been keeping an eye on the passing scene outside was urging us to look at the enthralling spectacle above the track. We scrambled up hastily, pushing our way out of the compartment, tripping over rucksack straps on the way - and there soaring into the sky just outside the window was my first stunning view of the Alps, white mantled and totally gobsmacking. I could hardly take my eyes off them, but there was something interesting going on down below as well in the vicinity of the track. Soldiers in uniform were marching up and down on the gravel, patrolling the area with submachine guns over their shoulders. They were guarding the Brenner Pass that provided a route through the Alps into Italy. Being slightly ignorant of things that had gone on in Europe during the Second World War I was taken aback, but it was of course only twenty years since the end of hostilities and there was animosity over the pass which the Italians were claiming as theirs, despite the fact that it used to belong to Austria. When I had been at school in England in the forties and fifties, history lessons seemed to dry up with Henry the Eighth. More up to date occurrences appeared to be brushed under the carpet, or maybe they were too sensitive.

We alighted in Bolzano at 2pm where Susan, Jane, Susie and I scrambled down onto the platform into the searing heat of the Italian summer sun, while the boys carried on to Trento to catch a bus for their venue in the Brenta region. We also had to catch a bus, to Canazei, from where we would walk in through the forest to the Sassolunga, but the first thing we had in mind was an ice cream shop. Never having been abroad before, the soaring temperature was totally unexpected and after purchasing large vanilla cones ('gelati' in Italian) we hurried to find a shaded park bench in the town and eat them quickly before they melted.

Next on the agenda was to find the bus station, but a shock awaited us there. It was Sunday afternoon and no buses for Canazei were operational until Monday morning! We had not bargained for this disaster and had no idea where we were going to spend the night in Bolzano, nor did we want to waste our limited finances on an expensive hotel. Cash to spend abroad was restricted in those days. You could only take £50 per person out the country, and that wouldn't go far on a three week climbing holiday if extravagances were added on. There were tales of mountaineers smuggling out extra paper notes wrapped in the coils of their climbing ropes, but we were too honest, or was it 'too scared' to do that!

We found a cool marble slab in the bus station and sat down, enjoying the chill of the marble against our hot sweaty hands, while we snapped at each other in an attempt to make an agreeable plan for the night ahead. The fact that we were tired from the journey didn't help and the best and cheapest idea we came up with was kipping under a bush in the park - but first of all we decided that a decent meal was called for. We walked back into the main part of the town and found an open air restaurant ornamented with vines where we sat down to await service. This wasn't as easy as we thought it was going to be as none of us could speak Italian, so it had to be done with sign language and gesticulation, pointing at things other diners were consuming, along with a nod of confirmation.

We attracted a lot of attention while we were dining, from an audience of zealous and eager Italian males, not all of it welcome. Four young British hiking girls, without chaperone, dressed in shorts, we were quickly finding out were just too much for the libido of the ardent Italian male and when we left the restaurant several of them followed us down the street. We went into a newsagents and bought an English/Italian phrase book, hastily looking up the Italian for 'Go away!' after which we shouted it at Italians about to make a nuisance of themselves, not always with the desired result.

Eventually we found the municipal park which was well endowed with benches, shady flowering bushes and trees, but we had no sooner sat down when we discovered we had several impassioned members of the Carabiniere in tow. They chattered to us excitedly in a mixture of Italian and German accompanied by suggestive signs and alluring smiles. Our repeated Italian 'Go away!' shouts had no effect, so we crossed the park off our list of possible places to spend the night and hurriedly walked back into the town centre.

We returned to the railway station which we thought might be too public a place to be propositioned, found the second class waiting room and dashed inside, closing the door behind us. We had it to ourselves after a few commuters vanished to board a train and it looked promising for a kip, with several high backed wooden benches. We re-arranged these, stowed our packs underneath, removed our boots and using our anoraks as pillows we stretched out for forty winks. It was quiet for a while and I was about to nod off when the door opened and a dapper little Italian appeared. Through half closed eyes I saw him sit down on the end of my bench, but I pretended to be asleep. Then next thing I knew he'd tweaked my toe. I sat up with a start and glared crossly at him, but undeterred by my resentment of his antics he began an animated recital in Italian. I shook my head and waved my hands dismissively. Could he not understand that I'd no idea what he was talking about, or maybe I had a pretty good idea, but decided the best plan was not to let on! It worked, because he gave up and started poking Jane instead, and he finished up with Susie, while Jane and I tried to suppress a snigger in the background.

Meanwhile railway personnel patrolling the platform outside had been looking in the window to see what was going on and noticing that we were attempting to kip in the waiting room overnight they frowned in disapproval. However, they were interrupted from doing anything about the situation because a train suddenly arrived and our annoying Italian dashed outside and jumped aboard. Phew! We suddenly had the place to ourselves again and the railway officials didn't return, so we settled down once more to catch up on further sleep.

We were vaguely aware of trains coming and going throughout the night and were wakened on occasions by ear splitting whistles and doors slamming. Other passengers came and went in the waiting room but none of them bothered us until the early hours of the morning when we were suddenly surprised at the appearance of a local policeman. Other passengers got up and disappeared, but we faked sleep until he tackled us with instructions that sounded like we were to clear off. Susan meanwhile was snoring loudly so we followed her example and he turned on his heel and left. After that I nodded off once again before suddenly jumping awake as the dawn was breaking and finding myself staring into the face of another displeased policeman, his immaculate uniform glinting with intimidating articles to contain any aggressive activity and protect his person. We got the message and hastily collecting our belongings we made off towards the bus station where we found their cafeteria was already open, which encouraged us to have two cups of coffee and doughnuts before catching the first bus for Canazei.

It was a two hour journey to reach our destination over some intimidating roads with sharp, hairpin bends, perpendicular drops, narrow gorges and glimpses of awe inspiring views through the forests. Canazei was a village in the heart of the Dolomites with a good selection of tourist shops, but we had to steel ourselves not to buy souvenirs at this stage of the holiday, as all extra purchases would have to be carried for its entirety. However, I did rise to a pair of sunglasses and a couple of postcards. We had tried our best to travel light with minimum spare clothing - one extra pair of trousers, shirt, shorts and a dress for special occasions, although when we were going to get that kind of special occasion I'd no idea. We also had swimming costumes and we shared out the carrying of maps, guide books, dixies, the stove, snack food and my climbing rope. We didn't have tents as we were intending to use the mountain huts and we were aware that they also served meals, which was helpful. The huts turned out to be a revelation as they were mainly substantial stone built properties several storeys high, some of which were situated in the most remote and inhospitable terrain, but as yet we were unaware of this phenomena.

From Canazei we were intending to take a track through the forest to reach the Sella Hut at the foot of the Sassolungo pinnacles, which we could see at this stage due to the forest. From the guide book it sounded like a simple matter to follow this track, but it was nothing of the kind. The path became devious as we climbed steeply uphill and the forest became thicker by the minute. In addition we were climbing at the hottest time of day, still trying to get accustomed to the weight of our packs, and to make matters worse every conceivable kind of disagreeable insect seemed to be making in our direction. We began to feel like boiled beetroot as we laboured and sweated through dense foliage, wondering if we had somehow lost the proper track. The way to the Sella Hut should surely be well beaten and decisive. An argument developed on who had picked this track and whose reading of the map had been inaccurate, but a glimmer of hope lay ahead when I spotted a clearing through the jungle.

Suddenly we burst out of the trees and found ourselves in an amazing Alpine meadow, boasting a tapestry of bright, eye-catching flowers and rolling hills of cropped verdant green grass. Above them lay acres of scree leading up to the three giant towers of the Sassolungo, sharply etched against the blue of the sky – real Dolomite peaks at last. I was completely spellbound. Here and there in the meadows below were attractive wooden chalets with wide overhanging roofs and balconies. The first one we passed was called the Valentino Hut and it appeared to sell refreshments to walkers so we hurried towards it and ordered beer with lemonade, which we drank thirstily on the terrace, savouring every drop. Although the Sella Hut was still some distance ahead, being able to see it boosted our morale.

It was late afternoon by the time we reached the hut, and discovered that it was a huge expansive chalet, built of stone and appearing more like a hotel than a climbers' hostel. We also discovered that a road ran past the front entrance with coaches parked outside, so we re-examined our map and realised that a twisting road on the far side of Canazei did actually go past the hut, but it had not been on our bus route. Anyway we were not on a coach tour. It was supposed to be a walking holiday!

We were completely taken aback by all the civilization and luxury of the hut which was supporting the tourist industry, but when we contacted the proprietor and asked for a room in the cheapest category, we found there were two huts! We were escorted across the road to an annex of much inferior décor and facilities. Nevertheless it was a bed for the night and after the last two, in the station waiting room and our overnight train, it was luxury. The annex was a stone cottage with squeaking bunks, cold water in the bathroom and no toilet paper in the loo. Nor was there a lock for the toilet door and men used the bothy in addition to women! We were not impressed!

In contrast to this the main building across the road was like a palace with prices to match, but we were allowed to use the dining room, bar and lounge at night. As it was too early for dinner we ordered ham rolls and coffee in the bar and wrote postcards. Dinner was served at 7pm and began with a massive selection of Hors d'oeuvres and continued with roast meats, a choice of veg and various desserts. We wondered if this was going to be standard in all the Dolomite huts, but we met with disappointment there. The cuisine and variety dropped considerably in the more remote huts and those not reached by any kind of motor road, which was most of them!

After dinner Susie paid a visit to the WC adjacent to the bar and managed to pinch some toilet paper for the annex! We asked her if she couldn't have got a lock as well! Owing to all the activities of the past few days we retired to our bunkhouse early, about 9 o'clock if I remember right, and especially in view of breakfast being served in the main building at 6am.

Breakfast was a continental menu with rolls and apricot jam and the coffee was somewhat tepid, possibly because we were late arriving in the dining room. We noticed there was a line of empty water bottles on the sideboard that other residents were adding to, so we fetched ours and placed them at the end of the line, assuming they would be filled with water, refreshing juice or coffee, for walkers and climbers on a day's expedition such as we were contemplating. The plan was to do a twelve mile circuit of the Sassolungo Pinnacles on a high level path at their base, after which we would have a second night at the hut before moving on to another area.

When we collected the water bottles they were not filled with water, juice or coffee. The contents appeared to be cold tea with a rash of tea leaves floating in it, amongst slices of lemon. I wasn't partial to tea at the best of times, let alone cold tea, so I wasn't very amused. Dolomite streams were also not recommended for drinking without water purification tablets.

The weather was looking disappointing after the previous day's searing heat and as we were now walking at a higher and more exposed level, over seven thousand feet, we were aware of a chilly wind blowing round the towers. We'd set off in shorts too, hoping to begin cultivating a tan, but there was fat chance of that as we inspected blue-tinged flesh with goose bumps. The path was easily followed after our debacle in the forest the day before and periodically the way was marked with numbers painted on a convenient stone, which corresponded with the numbers on our map. Once we had covered a fair distance we generated a degree of heat and we were even glad of the cold refreshing tea, accompanied by snacks of compressed dates and watched over by curious Alpine cattle. Some of them had bells round their necks reminding me of 'Heidi' in Switzerland, my favourite book at primary school. It was also a day for savouring the exhilarating landscape and the awesome nature of the lofty Dolomite terrain, which in Italy was quite different from the rest of the Alps. But there was another characteristic of the Dolomites that we still had to experience and which caught up with us just as we arrived back at the hut. This was sudden and torrential rain accompanied by deafening claps of thunder, which lasted only a few minutes before clearing away, leaving the ground steaming behind it, and clouds of vapour rising from the forests below. How unlike Scotland when a heavy drizzle could last all day!

Passing the time before dinner in the bar we had an unexpected laugh with four English lads who were on a mountaineering holiday. It was a relief to converse freely in English again as they recounted tales of the climbs they had accomplished and the people they had encountered, including a gentleman who had torn the pocket of his breeches during a difficult ascent and his travellers cheques had fluttered out his pocket, after which the party had spent the rest of the day trying to retrieve them, a drama that no one would want to repeat.

Dinner that night was a feast of roast beef, salad creamed and parsley potatoes, stuffed olives and chopped vegetables, the likes of which we didn't see for the rest of our holiday. Generally speaking the huts had no provision for cooking one's own meals. You were expected to buy the fare available at the hut, or cook your own outside the premises. Chianti was the standard drink for accompanying dinner - red or white - sold in carafes at six shillings each and was more popular than water as a thirst quencher. A carafe could last all night with several glasses each!

The following day we would be moving on to another area, deeper in the mountains and at the foot of the Dolomites highest peak, the Marmolata, which had a convenient hut at the foot of it called Contrin.

# 3

# MARMOLATA

Our route to the Marmolata region took us back through Canazei, where an instant decision was made to invade the local coffee shop, as it might be several days before such an opportunity arose again. From there we had a good hike on a well trodden, but steep double track, winding into the heart of the highest mountains in the Dolomites. Much of the initial stages were forested and insect life was abundant, particularly with a larger species of crawling and flying ant than I'd ever seen in the British Isles. This curtailed sit down stops on the grass, but the scenery opening out above the forest was enthralling.

The Contrin Hut was also impressive, being another substantial stone built property, like a Scottish mansion house, complete with conservatory overlooking the valley and a three storey separate annex adjacent. Four wheel drive vehicles delivered provisions, groaning up the steep track, but these were few and far between. On more difficult access tracks and paths in the Dolomites pack mules were used for the conveyance of essential supplies and some huts had access to a cable car or pulley arrangement down a cliff face. In emergency of course there was always the helicopter.

At the hut, as per usual, we made enquiries regarding the cheapest class of accommodation and this saw us marching across to the proverbial annex, which in many ways was superior to the annex at Sella. This one was several storeys in height and had dormitories with bunks and single beds in addition to a good washroom with an excellent view from the window. A member of staff showed us to our room on the second floor where Susie dumped her kit on a single bed, but when she sat on it the legs collapsed and she landed on the floor! We sniggered and propped it up again temporarily, just before the chambermaid returned with extra blankets, but when one of us leaned against it the whole thing collapsed for the second time with a resounding crash! After a moment's embarrassed silence we were all laughing and the maid dashed off giggling to fetch a hammer and nails!

Following this hilarity we had a couple of hours to wait before dinner was served in the main building, so we took our primus stove outside and brewed tea, accompanied by a packet of biscuits. We'd booked in for three nights as we intended to fully explore the area around the Marmolata, although the hut had such a spellbinding setting that we wondered if even three nights would give us enough time to see everything at close quarters. To start with there was the enticing peak we had seen from the bathroom window which looked doable even for our level of experience. It was referred to on the map as Vernardais and was accessed by a footpath.

Explorations round the back of the hut leading up to the Marmolata revealed an outdoor open ended chapel. Such Spartan constructions in either wood or stone, complete with bell and cross were commonplace in the Dolomites. Whether they were built to offer a place to pray for safety in the mountains, or for Sunday services we were not quite sure. The path that led to the Marmolata and the Ombretta Pass was directly beyond that, with a long green meadow in between, before giving way to scree, rock and snow. We reserved explorations in that direction for our second day in the area after tackling the Vernardais.

Dinner in the Contrin Hut was characterized by exceptionally slow service, with chief items on the menu being minestrone soup, followed by goulash and potatoes, with no desert being mentioned.
In the morning the breakfast rolls were tough, which fell in with the system that the more isolated the hut, the tougher was the bread, but we soon learned not to be fussy!

Our planned peak for the day was glittering in the morning sunlight, enticing us to get going without delay, but only three of us decided to tackle it, as Susie said she was spending the day sunbathing in the meadow. The rest of us set off on a winding scree path, which steepened as we gained height. The panorama in all directions was more exhilarating by the minute as we sweated up the steep track and almost had to scramble on the final slope to the summit. Having attained it we found another difference between Italy and Scotland. The summits of the mountains were marked by a stout wooden cross supported by wire hawsers, not a stone build cairn. We tried to photograph each other at the cross, but owing to the exceptionally brilliant Italian sun at high altitude we got the camera settings wrong, leading to colour drained, somewhat disappointing results!

Back at the hut in the late afternoon we boiled water for coffee outside on the primus and polished off a packet of biscuits from the hut shop. Shortly afterwards the weather suddenly deteriorated and with some time to wait for dinner we opted for a kip in the dormitory.

Dinner was a repetition of the previous night except that we managed to procure a desert, but not without hassle. To begin with the waitress who only spoke Italian and German couldn't understand our request, and Susie's schoolgirl German was also unproductive. We finished up drawing a cake decorated with cherries on a piece of paper, but it was mistaken for a clock. The second cake we drew was mistaken for a fancy hat until Jane took over the artistry and drew a slice of cake, leading to the appearance of an apple tart, so we settled for that.

After dinner a cloudburst commenced outside, sending down such volumes of water we thought we were going to be flooded out. Crossing over from the main building to the annex was like plunging through a river. Shortly after the deluge ceased a number of large walking and climbing parties descended on the hut, many of them German, and all of them soaked to the skin. The Germans sat in the lounge in the main building all evening, singing lustily and entertaining on the mouth organ, so we had a grand sociable night with them.

Despite the very hot daytime temperatures in Italy, interspersed at times with violent thunderstorms, the nights could be extremely chilly and snow still clung to the upper slopes of the mountains. The exterior grandeur of the huts also disguised some decided short comings within, one of which was usually no hot water in the bathroom, and Contrin was one of them. Hair washing in freezing cold water was quite a chore and we learned not to do it at night with no drying facilities.

The following day dawned clear and sunny. We didn't have enough experience and equipment to climb the impressive Marmolata, but we decided to investigate the lower slopes and maybe have a look at the entrance to the Ombretta Pass nearby. This involved walking up the valley first which was hot work. A decision was made to halt for sunbathing in the long grass, in our shorts and T-shirts, with liberal amounts of sun cream plastered over exposed flesh. I felt obliged to join the others, but every so often I wriggled round restlessly to scan the horizon through the tinted glass of my shades. 'What kind of mountaineering holiday was this?' I mused crossly. I was becoming aware of the fact that my aspirations for this holiday might not coincide with those of my walking companions. Well no one was going to curtail my desire to explore this fantastic new mountain terrain. I made a decision.

"I'm going up to the head of the pass, to the lower slopes of the Marmolata," I announced, and without waiting on a reply I made ready to go.

They looked at me sleepily through half closed eyes and shouted after me, "Don't be long then."

I felt slightly irritated. I was an adult, not a child. Ever since I could walk I had this strong urge to explore and sunbathing was not on my agenda. How could they just lie there ignoring all this amazing stuff? With my anorak tied round my waist and my camera slung over my shoulder I made speed up to the head of the valley.

After clearing the meadow I tramped on through rising fields of scree and snow at the base of the Marmalata, taking a route that led away from the path, until the terrain became much steeper and more demanding. It was at this stage that I decided to cut back into the pass and see what was on the other side. The higher I climbed the more enticing were the mountain ridges popping up over the horizon, which like a drug encouraged me to keep going until I reached the top of the pass. I was sorely tempted to carry on over the other side where I could just make out another hut in the distance, but I knew I had to go back, as I'd already been away longer than I had intended. Despite my aspirations I knew that as a group there was protocol and limitations, but I also knew that in later years I could come back.

I bounded down the path into the valley and found my sunbathing companions where I had left them. "You missed yourselves!" I said, as Susan raised herself on one elbow. She agreed to come back to the head of the pass with me, but suggested we had a snack of dates and Creamola Foam first.

The others stayed where they were while Susan and I climbed steadily to the head of the pass. We looked at the other hut just visible in the distance but there was no time to go investigating in that direction, just to have to retrace our footsteps in the time we had available, and possibly missing dinner at Contrin into the bargain! Instead we decided to explore a dugout cave in the rock on the Marmolata side of the pass. We peered into the gloom within and during this manoeuvre Susan dropped her sun glasses inside. Squeezing through the opening we rummaged around in the darkness until we found them, and by this time our eyes were accustomed to the light, so we had a better look round. It was during this exercise that we noticed another opening into the interior, with a path leading beyond it.

We moved forward through the opening to investigate, but the atmosphere quickly became charged with a tingling suspense and something not particularly inviting. There were shadows moving along the walls and water was dripping, making a steady plopping sound. Then we saw a crack in the rock face ahead and something that looked suspiciously like two fingers caught in the opening!

We jumped and squealed in alarm as we hastily backed away,

tumbling back out the main entrance into the sunlit pass, blinking like startled owls. Whether it was a rubber glove, or whether it was human we hadn't waited to find out. We had a suspicion that people hid in the dugouts during the war and it was rumoured that many people tried to escape through the passes. It was a chilling thought. We descended the pass to the meadows below considerably shaken by the experience and trying to convince each other that what we had seen was only a discarded glove!

In the evening our party were complaining of sunburn despite the lashings of sun cream applied and even I had not escaped, although I had been more active on the slopes. After dinner I washed a pair of thick woollen climbing socks, but it was a couple of days before they were completely dried, which was a lesson learned.

The hut was quiet in the evening in contrast to the previous night's lusty singing parties, but instead we were entertained by a young man and a chambermaid, both employed to work at the hut during the summer. They were playing a noisy game of cards, characterized by the loser in each game having to carry out a forfeit, which involved all kinds of antics, from refilling our water jug and hopping round the stove to dashing into the kitchen to fetch soup ladles, or up the stairs to the bathroom for a couple of bath brushes!

Next morning we would be on the move again with a long walk through the mountains to the iconic Vajolet Towers in the Rosengarten area and a night on the way at the Caimpedie Hut above the village of Pozza.

# 4

# THE VAJOLET TOWERS

Our next venue was one of the major regions in the Dolomites for climbers known as the Rosengarten which housed the imposing eminences of Catinaccio and the Vajolet Towers. To reach it on foot from the Contrin Hut we planned a two day walk-in with an overnight stop on route at another hut called Caimpedie.

The day started on a high with good mountain paths and splendid views, but after crossing a main road at the village of Pozza we entered extensive forestry plantations and promptly got lost. The path we had selected for approaching Caimpedie was poorly marked and devious, twisting and turning between the trees as we ploughed slowly uphill, sweating in the sultry heat, swiping at flying ants and stepping over large black beetles crawling underfoot. Several times we wondered if we were still headed in the right direction, but a solitary woodcutter we chanced upon confirmed it was correct.

It was a long slog to clear the forest and late afternoon before we finally caught sight of our objective. Caimpedie was a sturdy stone building with an expansive terrace, where much to our astonishment crowds of tourists were relaxing in deck chairs sipping refreshments. On closer inspection we were certain that never in a million years had they walked up to the hut by the route we had taken.

"Where on earth have all those people come from?" we queried, completely gobsmacked. Apart from the woodcutter we hadn't passed a living soul on the path and the people lounging on the terrace admiring the view across the valley didn't appear to be long distance walkers. However, when we rounded the corner of the hut all was suddenly revealed. There was a cable car not far away which was ferrying people up and down the mountain from Pozza! How we had missed that we didn't know, because it would have saved a great deal of time and hassle and probably enabled us to reach the Rosengarten in one day! The only thing we had saved was the expense but we felt obliged to remember that we were on a walking holiday, not a tourist package!

As soon as the sun dipped below the horizon the crowds started to disperse, leaving only the walkers and climbers in the dining room in the evening. The cuisine was rather lacking in variety, but we couldn't see a valid excuse for this, seeing as provisions could be dispatched by cable car on a daily basis. As there was no annex attached to the premises we were housed in the main building for once, but in contrast to our previous accommodation there was no electricity, with lighting being supplied by candles. The dormitory had a couple of candles in holders on a wooden shelf, but as there were none in the washroom you had to carry one from the dormitory along the corridor, shielding its flickering flame in case it went out before you arrived.

After breakfast the intention had been to move on through the forest in the direction of the Rosengarten and the Vajolet Hut, but just as we were about to leave there were ominous rumbles overhead, followed by torrential rain, so we decided to wait until it abated and occupy the interval playing cards in the dining room. None of the day trippers of the previous day reappeared, possibly having been put off by the low cloud cover and lashing rain. Around mid day however, there was a sudden transformation with the sun breaking through and clouds of sizzling steam issuing from damp foliage in the forest. It was time to make a move.

Compared to the long uphill grind of the day before our route was now like a walk in the park, with a superior, broad track and table and bench sets along the way, where we could relax and have a snack. At intervals we came upon a clearing with several chalets, even a shop and café, and there were other Land Rover tracks branching off at junctions, winding downhill, possibly towards Pozza. It was totally confusing, making us realise we had not interpreted the map to our best advantage.

Eventually we left the chalets and the forest behind and found ourselves approaching the Rosengarten with its majestic, grandiose towers of barren rock. On our left was now the huge bulk of Cattinacio, the highest eminence in the region with a sheer cliff face of massive proportions sweeping up above the remaining trees, while ahead of us was another cliff, lower and broken into buttresses, around which our path appeared to zigzag steeply. A chalet was etched against the skyline and we wondered if it was our accommodation at the Vajolet Hut, but unfortunately it wasn't. It was a private concern, while our quarters were further back in the centre of a barren stony basin surrounded by the grandest amphitheatre of rock architecture I'd ever seen. It was totally different from both the Sassolunga area and the Marmalata making us feel like we'd arrived on a futuristic film set on another planet, devoid of vegetation. The three Vajolet Towers with their impressive spires dominated the region, while other lesser spires, lofty knife edge ridges, massive buttresses and gullies full of mysterious shadows were almost too numerous to take in. I wanted to run around and explore everything at once, but first of all we had to book into our accommodation.

Our hut was the only other building located on the plateau, while the high limestone towers frowned down upon us from above. As we approached our accommodation a man dashed out to greet us and hung around while we signed in at the office, then he promptly offered to escort us to our quarters which were in the annex next door. We didn't know if he was a guide or a hut employee, but we soon became aware that he was neither! He led us up a narrow rickety wooden staircase to our room which contained four double bunks in a small dimly lit apartment with a bench alongside the wall opposite. We sat down on the bench and started to unpack, but our man also sat down and watched us, seeming to be in no hurry to depart. He chattered incessantly in Italian, gesturing with his hands and smiling alluringly, being quite undeterred by our lack of interest in his conduct. Having unpacked our stuff we wanted to stretch out on the bunks and relax before dinner, but something had to be done

Vajolet Towers
Rosengarten

VAJOLET
HUT

about our irritating visitor.

We remembered the Italian for 'go away' and repeated it several times to no avail, by which time we were all simmering in annoyance. Although he seemed to get the general message and reluctantly moved towards the door his departure didn't quite materialize, for there was still shuffling noises outside. When we heard retreating footsteps on the staircase we bolted the door, but not ten minutes later he was back, hammering on it with his fists and calling out beseeching remarks. His intentions were obvious so we made a hurried plan, threw the door open with a flourish and indicated that we were going to report him to the manager of the hut! He must have understood, because he backed off at that point, and as we clattered down the staircase he took flight ahead of us, disappearing out a side door and fleeing across the valley at top speed! Fortunately the threat of the hut manager had produced results because it was the last we saw of him.

At dinner we discovered that the price was escalating again, due to difficulties in accessing supplies, which had to be ferried up the cliff by an ingenious pulley system. This also affected variety, but I have to say the minestrone soup with lashings of parmesan cheese was very tasty, while the fried eggs with spaghetti which we choose to follow were not! If one had plenty money to spend, the roast meat dishes looked appetizing, but meanwhile we were trying to economize until we saw how far our finances were going to stretch.

As climbers moved between the huts we tended to meet up with people we had seen before and on this occasion we met up with the English lads we'd seen at Sella. The atmosphere in the huts was eclectic with a mixture of jovial banter, singing, route discussions, examination of technical rock gear and consuming of much Chianti from carafes on the tables.

It wasn't until we retired to the dormitory for the night that things started to go pear-shaped again. In our absence four young men from Switzerland had been allocated the bunks underneath us, there being no separate dorms for men and women in these establishments. There was no repetition of our previous odd man's behaviour, but they were out for a bit of boisterous hilarity, which began with them catching hold of our toes as we jumped onto the top bunks and bouncing us up and down with their feet underneath our mattresses! Telling them to cut it out, only increased their activities, before they discovered Susie's shampoo bottle and started throwing that around, playing catch, and calling out loudly – 'Shampo-o-o' obviously being intrigued with the name. Nevertheless peace eventually reigned and as they were all hard climbers intent on some demanding vertical route the following day they reluctantly clambered into their bunks and silence reigned, only punctuated occasionally by a subdued snigger.

The following morning they rose unsociably early and made a great deal of noise collecting their climbing gear, banging the dormitory door and clomping down the wooden staircase outside. Having been thoroughly wakened up by all that activity it wasn't long before we got up ourselves and went down to the dining room to see what was on offer for breakfast. The rolls were less tough than those supplied at Caimpedie, but for some reason the coffee was disgusting and even the smell of it had us removing our cups to another table, before going outside to brew our own tea on the primus.

The plan for the day was to explore the Rosengarten area, beginning with a steep ascent of the high, barren valley opposite which led to the base of the Vajolet Towers. It was actually more a scramble, rather than a rock climb, but we took the rope with us in case of unforeseen difficulty. Unfortunately the weather deteriorated when we arrived in close proximity to the towers, which curtailed the view as swathes of mist descended and cloaked the pinnacles and the climbers involved in ascents. Instead of waiting on the mist to clear for a photo shoot or glimpse of the climbers inching their way upwards, we carried on to a higher level behind the bulk of Catinaccio where there was a small wooden hut, called Santner. I was amazed to see a building in such an inhospitable place and selling a variety of refreshments. It was situated at 9,000 feet and had a terrace outside with deck chairs. The setting was spellbinding, with Cattinacio rearing upwards on one side and a sheer drop opposite with an expansive Dolomite view just emerging beneath the mist, while on our right there were glimpses between wraithlike clouds of the majestic, awesome towers. We bought drinks which cost a fortune and sipped them on the terrace while waiting for the mist to disperse.

Not far from the hut, close to the rear of Cattinacio, was reputed to be a via ferrata route known as the Rosengarten Path, which followed a circuit back to the Vajolet Hut. It was not for the faint hearted and included ladders, fixed ropes and pitons to facilitate progress over sheer drops and difficult, exposed rock terrain. I was keen to have a look at the route and perhaps try it out, but my companions were not interested. Eventually I persuaded them to have a look at the beginning of it which swept abruptly down a wall of damp rock into a bottomless gully full of misty gloom. They recoiled at the very thought of setting foot on it, especially in less than perfect weather conditions, so the decision was made to leave it until the following day, when we could perhaps have another look.

We retraced our steps to the Santner hut where we now had a good view of the Vajolet Towers, mostly clear of mist. Parties of climbers were inching their way up the knife edge of the nearest pinnacle which was mind blowing, although Dolomite rock was reputed to be abundant in holds. The downside was the massive exposure below and the perpendicular gradient, with the only way of getting back to base being to abseil. We shivered at the thought of tackling something so perilous, but the parties battling their way to the tops were obviously enjoying themselves, because we heard singing and yodelling floating down from the heights, including 'The Bonnie Banks of Loch Lomond' - so we presumed some of them were Scots. The Dolomites I had discovered was a favourite place amongst Scottish mountaineers.

On returning to the hut I discovered that one of my thick woollen climbing socks that I'd left to dry on the dormitory window sill in the morning had fallen overboard and was now reposing on the roof of an outhouse below. To rescue it required a considerable feat of mountaineering skill and a mantelshelf to finish onto the roof, which was quite the most energetic and technical accomplishment of the day.

We had several hours to wait until dinner and feeling like a snack before that we decided to try and obtain one from the kitchen, with a roll and fried sausage being the most popular decision, but the chef needless to say had limited English and our request had him bamboozled. Nevertheless, he obligingly opened the larder and produced assorted items, holding each up in turn for inspection, which was hilarious but unproductive. The nearest to what we had in mind was a giant sausage, but we settled for it sliced on bread.

In the evening the hut was packed as a thunderstorm had swelled the numbers who were taking shelter and ordering meals, making the already slow service diabolical, not to mention even getting a seat. We squeezed onto a table end in the bar opposite some French guys, whereupon Susan and Susie immediately struck up a conversation in French, which I found extremely boring, my school girl French not being up to translating it. After our meal the French were replaced with Austrians and a guitar which was much more entertaining.

Our Swiss dormitory companions also returned, all soaked to the skin after being caught in an early evening downpour and when we retired for the night we found the room full of strings of wet clothes, puddles on the floor and the steamy odour of damp wool and leather. The hut bathroom also had its failings in this establishment, as there were no plugs in the wash basins and the toilet had no seat. To replace it there was a shallow porcelain tray on the floor with a hole at one end and a marked space to place the feet. One was expected to squat in the middle of the porcelain tray before pulling a chain to flush, then quickly jumping out of the way as a pool of water swirled vigorously and finally gurgled down the hole.

Talk about primitive!

On the following day there was a decided improvement in the weather. It had been agreed to try a circuit of the via ferrata path round Cattinacio, but in the end only Jane was persuaded to tackle it, as the others had opted for sunbathing outside the hut. I was gobsmacked, having thought we were on a mountaineering holiday, not a Mediterranean sunbathing enterprise!

Jane and I left them to it and set off for the Via Ferrata from the opposite direction to what we had inspected the day before from the Santner hut. I always thought it was easier to climb up, rather than down and this certainly proved to be the case. The route from this direction was relatively easy for a via ferrata, although it contained some unexpected surprises including the fixed ropes and ladders, adding a touch of adrenalin and excitement, as did the breath taking views below. Having regained the Santner Hut we paused beside it for a while before descending and meeting Susan who had decided to come up and find us.

In the evening, which was our last one in the area, we arrived early in the dining room and grabbed a decent seat, as well as prompt service of minestrone. There was a party of Italians at the other end of our table who consumed gallons of red wine all evening, with their behaviour getting noisier and more exuberant as the night progressed. They were obviously exchanging jokes which none of us could comprehend due to the language barrier, so we retired early to pack up for our move the next day back to Bolzano, before going on to the Brenta region by train and bus.

In the morning we shouldered our packs, paid our bill and started to descend the track to the lower valleys and the forests when who did we meet but Ronnie, the leader of the Langside. He said that some of the boys had arrived with him late the previous night and they were dossing underneath a boulder beside the track, which was a popular howff nick named the 'Grossen Stein' by Scotsmen wanting to do things on the cheap. They had become disillusioned with bad weather at the Brenta so half of them had decided to come over to the Rosengarten in search of more promising conditions. As we were headed that way this was not news that we really wanted to hear!

Ronnie invited us to sit on the rocks outside their accommodation and chat about what we had been doing before we headed off, and when we told him of our lengthy forest debacle on the way up via Caimpedie he advised a shortcut that led directly to Pozza.

Having taken this on board we were relieved to catch an earlier bus to Bolzano, where the plan was to stay overnight in the local youth hostel. But plan's can go astray because we couldn't find the hostel and we ended up in a guest house run by nuns. The upside of this was that it supplied lashings of hot water so we all took advantage of this and washed our hair.

# 5

# BRENTA

After our comfortable night in the nuns' guest house we caught a train in the morning to Trento which was anything but comfortable, having wooden bench seats all facing forward in rows like a bus. We were relieved we were only travelling forty miles.

Trento turned out to be a sizeable town with good shops, restaurants and a swimming pool so we decided to book two nights in the local youth hostel, which might also give the Brenta weather a chance to improve. The hostel was some distance away on the edge of town and having arrived there at 4 o'clock we were told it didn't open until six. Fortunately we were allowed to leave our packs, after which we walked back into the town in search of a decent restaurant to get a meal which offered something other than either minestrone or spaghetti. Despite the excellent minestrone served in Italy it was time for a change, which led to scrutinising the menu displayed outside various premises, mini dictionary in hand, and having seen a different soup we dashed inside and ordered it. Delivery of the soup however led to stunned silence as we saw the pool of brown meat Consommé with a raw egg floating in the middle of it, sunny side up, like a desert island. Soup spoons were hastily grabbed as we tried to fish out the sunny islands before they broke up, which gave rise to a great deal of hilarity, while at the next table four guys were having equal hilarity trying to eat extra long strips of spaghetti dripping in tomato sauce. We got chatting to them and discovered that they were also to be staying in the hostel, which sorted out the evening entertainment, along with cards, wine and Italian television.

The hostel was different is some respects from those in Britain, in that both sexes shared the same bathroom which wasn't very conducive to having a thorough wash - and the toilet paper was sheets of torn up newsprint. Talk about doing things on the cheap!

Our full day in Trento was spent looking round the shops and the municipal park, before going on to the swimming pool in the afternoon, which was well worth it for the hot showers!

In the evening, with our spaghetti eating companions having moved on, we were stuck with Italian television minus sub titles, until a guy arrived with a guitar slung over his shoulder. He was also Italian but we got the warden to persuade him to come to the common room with his guitar and provide some entertainment. Fortunately he agreed and was soon joined by another on a mouth organ, and a couple of French, whose contribution to the scene was rhythmic beating with hands and fists on table tops, accompanied by whistling and other explosive, guttural noises.

Next morning we rose early, packed up and headed for the bus station, arriving there to miss the first bus for Madonna di Campiglio by two minutes. We had two hours to wait for the next one, during which interval I visited a local newsagents and bought a harmonica which I proceeded to try out in the waiting room at the station, with faint signs of disapproval from my companions as I tried to figure out the suck and blow technique for 'The Bonnie Banks of Loch Lomond!'

Our conveyance left at 11 o'clock and the latter part of our journey was a hair-raising ride as we climbed steeply round fearsome hairpin bends, hoping the vehicle had good brakes. Sometimes we looked straight down into deep green lakes and at other times the gradient was so precipitous that you couldn't see what was below. I was glad we were going up and not down, then suddenly we arrived in a bus park where we had to change for the Campiglio service in the heart of the mountains.

By the time we arrived at our destination it was 2pm and we had a long walk ahead of us to reach the Brenta Hut where we would be staying for several days. Thinking it might be a good idea to get a few grocery items before leaving we headed for the nearest store and on the way met one of our club boys on a similar mission. He was one of the few who had elected to stay behind at the Brenta waiting for decent climbing weather, and he described the diabolical conditions they had been inflicted with, including snow and hail, which had seen morale drop to rock bottom. However, as it was one of the best climbing areas in the Dolomites some of them were doggedly hanging on. We listened with some apprehension, but we were already committed so we were heading up regardless.

Our main aim for the visit was to have a look at the famous Bochette high level path, which was a via ferrata of more extreme proportions to the one at the Rosengarten that Jane and I had completed. I had my doubts as to whether my companions would be willing to tackle it, and in the present prevailing weather this looked like being even less likely.

It took us three hours to reach the Brenta Hut, laden with all our gear, including loaves of bread, butter and jam from the village store. Despite the damp conditions it was hot, tiring work climbing uphill on the rough sandy path threading the forest environment, before reaching barren, rock strewn terrain at a higher level. Tendrils of mist were draped round the peaks appearing above us, obscuring most of the view, but a plus point was the absence of insect life.

The four storey hut with shutters at the windows and a terrace at the front was situated in a spectacular, elevated, vantage point, surrounded by a grand circle of perpendicular rock rearing skywards, part of which was cloud wreathed. Our quarters were in the attic, in two and three tier bunks and the bathroom was next door with a lino floor that always seemed to be wet. The dining room on the ground floor doubled as a common room and the view from the windows, when you could see it, was dramatic.

We ordered the traditional minestrone soup and a sweet omelette to follow, and found the soup very tasty, while the sweet omelette was not, although it did have a taste, two dominant ones in fact, these being black currant jam and salt. I was stuck after two forkfuls, but Susan professed to enjoy it and said she'd buy mine off me!

Our club boys who had remained in the area were not actually staying in the hut although they used the common room and sometimes ordered meals. They had done a deal with the hut manager and had the use of a small out house nearby which they were dossing in. Whether they had it's use for free or a nominal sum I wasn't quite sure, but after having seen it I thought it was debateable whether they or the other half of their party who were sleeping beneath the rock in the Rosengarten were the most uncomfortable!

At the Brenta the boys were always in the hut in the evening booking a decent seat and a bottle of Chianti, and they were invariably keen for a few games of solo with our cards. The hut was situated at six thousand feet and the area seemed to be making its own weather, quite unlike what we had experienced elsewhere in the Dolomites. Nevertheless the premises was extremely busy, owing to the area's reputation for serious rock climbing routes, but patience was wearing thin for some of those who had been forced indoors for days. They were waiting on a break and some were getting to the stage of risking even semi decent weather for a dash across to the spires opposite the hut.

The day after our arrival there was no improvement and during breakfast we watched as sleet outside continually washed across the windows accompanied by a strong wind. Well we were not going anywhere! We decided to amuse ourselves inside the hut. There was a large pile of Alpine Journals in the bookcase so we helped ourselves to a few to look through the stunning Alpine photographs. Playing cards and writing materials came out again later and we watched as other disenchanted, grounded climbers read books, scribbled in notepads, inspected gear or studied maps. One guy was sitting with a jar of blackcurrant jam, methodically digging out the contents with a sticky teaspoon, in between scowling out the window at a blanket of impenetrable mist.

We ordered repeated coffees and finished off our cakes and bread from Campiglio, before remembering the game of dares that had taken place at the Contrin Hut. We inveigled the good looking Italian waiter called Oreste and one of the chambermaids to join in and we made up a box of dares, then a huge amount of hilarity erupted as we worked our way through them, dashing all over the hut - sliding down the banisters, pulling the overhead cistern chains, trying on hats and socks hanging to dry at the stove, emptying waste paper baskets and rearranging the cutlery and condiments in the dining room, to name a few of the items. Things however came to a halt when the hut manager appeared, reprimanding his staff for getting involved and glaring at the rest of us.

In the late afternoon the sleety rain turned to snow, which was building up to a fair covering outside and at six o'clock it was almost knee deep. Imagine a snowstorm in the Italian summer? We were awestruck. Venturing outside for the first time that day we waded through the snow to visit the boys in the outhouse. They were busy making a pot of Irish stew and potatoes on a couple of primus stoves, but they promised to join us in the hut later for a card session.

The following day it was neither snowing nor raining and the mist had lifted, but it was still exceptionally dull and grey. Nevertheless we decided we had to get out and do something, even if it was only a walk up to the head of the pass. We held a committee meeting round the breakfast table, which ended up with Susan and I arranging to walk up the valley towards one of the starting points for the Bochette path, to have a look at its feasibility. Meanwhile Jane and Susie opted for a shopping spree in Campiglio to get fresh bread, cream buns and doughnuts. Considering it would be two hours for the descent to the village and about three back up again, it was a long haul for the sake of a few sweet bakery items! The path to the village was completely unsuitable for motor transport of any description, but basic catering supplies for the hut were collected by mules with wooden panniers, driven down the valley by young lads employed at the hut.

Snow melt was dripping from the eaves as Susan and I left to explore the pass, beginning with a visit to the chapel nearby. Walking uphill from there we were ploughing through slush, but as we gained height the snow was crisp and deeper, with numerous unexpected holes between the rocks, almost waist deep. Reaching the head of the pass we looked down the other side to more of the same, before scouting about for a sign of the Bochette and any steel ladders.

There was a sheer cliff on our left and about a third of the way up was a narrow ledge fringed with snow. Maybe that was the path and if it was, there must be a ladder? Then we saw it, only vaguely detectable against the dark grey of the rock. We made our way towards it over slippery snow covered boulders, until we arrived at the bottom of the cliff and looked upwards, following the course of the ladder, which was the longest I'd ever seen. Thoughts of climbing up the cliff wall on this well worn perpendicular metal staircase was daunting to say the least, but I agreed to suss it out and asked Susan if she could take a photo from below.

I had a rush of adrenalin as I climbed, with the lust for adventure kicking in. The thought that part of the ladder could be rusted, have rungs missing, or worse, wall attachments coming adrift, didn't occur to me. Even thinking about it now, fifty years later I quail at what we did without any thought for safety!

When I arrived at the ledge this was the difficult part, transferring from the top rung of the ladder to the outwardly sloping, narrow path above, part covered in ice and snow, but fortunately there was a protruding rock nearby that could be grabbed while hoisting myself onto the path. By this time Susan was already started on the ladder below and was coming up to join me. Once on the ledge it was not too bad if one hugged the cliff wall and in some parts there was a steel handrail. The path was only a few feet wide and snow melt water was constantly dripping onto it from above. Having of necessity to avoid the outer edge which tumbled into the formidable depths below, we clung to the inner section and consequently caught more of the descending water. Progressing carefully we eventually reached a corner where it followed the contours of a gully set into the cliff with a deep abyss below. At this point it was hewn out of the rock with a roof of sorts above. "How about a photo holding up the roof?" I shouted to Susan, lifting my ice axe in a salute with my free hand.

As our path contoured around the lofty pinnacles searing above us we were never sure what to expect next and whether some insurmountable obstacle would send us back the way we had come, endeavouring to locate the top of the ladder that would lead us back to safety. We were too cock sure of ourselves, because the insurmountable obstacle arrived quicker than we had expected. Things were already getting dodgy when we came upon a section where the path had fallen away leaving a gap over thin air, bridged with a piton for use as a foothold, followed by another gap where a wooden plank had been inserted. We had to trust these makeshift repairs and hold our breath.

After that came a steep downward plunge with awkward and uneven rock steps hugging the cliff wall and a wire hawser handrail attached to the face, which I kept in a firm grip. At the bottom of this section a large gap was suddenly revealed, occupied by a sheer almost vertical, snow filled gully, dropping away for thousands of feet, with no obvious means to cross to the other side. We looked at the snow in dismay and we looked at each other. To cross the gap would involve cutting a path in the snow with our ice axes and we had no crampons. A slip could be fatal.

We sat down on one of the rock steps to consider our position. We were stumped, but just before we started to retrace our steps two figures appeared from the opposite side. They too stopped at the gully and hesitated. It was obvious that no one had crossed the gap for a number of days. We shouted across the gap to the two men and quickly discovered that they spoke English which was very helpful, so we asked about the path from their end, which they said was doable with care, but they were not prepared to proceed without a rope. We also had no rope with us as we had not intended to go so far, but we made a decision to try again the following day from the opposite end.

During our shouted conversation with the men they also told us about an accident that had occurred on the Campanile Basso, a lofty, challenging tower on the other side of the valley. A couple had been benighted during a climb the previous day and one had died of exposure. The mountain rescue had arrived on the scene and there was a lot of activity going on as the rescue was co-ordinated. We shivered at this information and decided that the sooner we got down from the Bochette the better, before we had an accident ourselves.

Retracing our steps was easier than the outward journey into the unknown, but we had a dicey moment locating the whereabouts of the ladder from above, then gingerly inching and sliding over the edge onto the first rung. From there on we felt a lot safer and once back in the valley we found the summer snow was rapidly receding and we were able to put speed on back to the hut, where we were looking forward to a substantial dinner. There was no sign of the mountain rescue at that point and Jane and Susie were still not back from Campiglio with the shopping. It was after six o'clock before they arrived, reporting that there was a stretcher now lying outside, with a body strapped to it. Presumably it was the culmination of the rescue on Campanile Basso, but we didn't want to go outside and look.

Instead we inspected the messages that Jane and Susie spread out on the table, including a smashed pot of peach jam and a greasy paper bag full of soggy doughnuts. For dinner we decided to bypass the spaghetti dishes and the sweet omelette fiasco of our first night, ordering instead Vitello Arrosto, which was a meat dish and rather more expensive. Our sweet course was supposed to comprise the doughnuts, but we ended up selling most of them to the club boys for half price, after sprinkling sugar on them to increase their appeal.

As the following day would be our last opportunity to complete the traverse of the Bochette path I was determined it was going to be accomplished. Even the weather was brilliant in the morning, and the snow in the vicinity of the hut had finally melted. Susan was also keen to try the path again from the opposite direction, so if we were thwarted at the gully at least we could say we'd done both ends. I took my climbing rope in case.

Instead of the one exceedingly long ladder to reach the cliff path as before, on this occasion it was several shorter ones with a rock scramble inbetween and when we reached the designated path we found that the weather improvements had brought out a fair number of other high level walking parties with a head for exposure. Some of these we had to pass from the opposite direction, which was a tricky procedure in respect of the width of the path. Due to the language barrier we didn't pick up any information about the bad step in the snow-filled gully either, which had stopped us in our tracks the day before, but the fact that they were passing us by indicated they had done the whole thing.

When we reached the gully we found that a fixed rope had been rigged up to facilitate crossing and a deep path had been beaten out in the snow, which simplified things considerably and took the sting out of the route, which was either a good or a bad thing, depending on how one looked at it! The water that had been dripping from above on the first section we'd previously done was also decreasing and there was less snow and ice on the ledge. Finally locating the longer ladder down to the high valley we were ecstatic at having completed this classic Dolomite route, which made a fitting end to the holiday.

Returning to the hut later in the afternoon we spent time relaxing on the terrace, along with Jane and Susie, playing a game of bowls and sunbathing before dinner. The area was completely transformed in the sunshine, and with it came a lifting of morale amongst the climbing fraternity. In the evening the common room was buzzing and a rousing folk singing session was taking precedence, accompanied by percussion with the dining room spoons and thumping of table tops.

The day after our exhilarating Bochette experience it was depressing to be packing up and heading home, but before our departure we persuaded our favourite hut staff to come out and pose for photographs. The walk back to Campiglio laden with gear took us most of the morning and when we arrived we were just in time to catch a bus with connections for Bolzano. It was so packed to begin with that we had to sit on the back step where there was no view of the fantastic scenery we were passing through. All we saw was a row of feet, boots, shoes, stockings, trouser legs, shopping bags and backpacks on the floor!

When we arrived in Bolzano in the late afternoon we managed to find the youth hostel we'd failed to locate before and booked in for two nights. It was neither as expensive nor as salubrious as the nun's guest house and appeared to be an old cinema in the process of conversion, with scaffolding everywhere, hammering, banging and clouds of dust. We were decidedly unamused at the situation, but as we were not expecting to spend much time in the building we agreed to stay. That was before we saw the bathroom! The toilet doors neither locked nor shut and the wash basin was a knee level trough with no plug and one cold water tap! Just right for cows, we smirked.

In the morning there was no long lie due to workmen hammering on the stairs so we got up earlier than intended. We inspected our remaining provisions for a quick breakfast, but the butter was rancid, the bread hard and our remaining pot of jam fell off a chair and smashed when someone accidentally tripped over the chair legs. We still had a tin of luncheon meat but it refused to budge from the tin and vigorous efforts to dislodge it suddenly had disastrous results. The meat flew onto the floor into the stour underneath Susan's bed before anyone could catch it! We went out for breakfast.

Our day was divided between shopping and swimming at an attractive open air lido, and after that we split up to do individual shopping with remaining Italian money before our return to Britain the following day. Ever since we'd arrived in the Dolomites I'd been admiring the Tyrolean peasant dresses worn by many of the women, characterized by wide skirted pinafores in alpine flower print on a dark background, along with white puckered low neck, short sleeved blouse and a dusky pink apron. It was completely out of character for me to want something so feminine, in exchange for my climbing apparel, and in a weak moment on my own I dashed into a dress outfitters and tried a few on. What the Italian assistant thought I'm not quite sure as I was obviously a hiking, backpacking Brit. Although it didn't occur to me at the time I was emulating the American male tourist in the Highlands of Scotland who must have a cheap kilt to parade in the street and take home to America, reminding him of his magical Highland holiday. I just had enough money for the dress and before I knew it, I had it in a plastic bag and was hurrying up the street to the youth hostel to put it on.

The rest of my party raised their eyebrows as I twirled in front of them in the dormitory and insisted on wearing it for our last night out on the town in Bolzano. I was chuffed to look like a girl from the Alps, but it wasn't long before I began to notice something odd. Jane, Susan and Susie received the usual wolf whistles and beseeching looks from the Italian males we passed by, but I was completely ignored! I came to the conclusion that it had to do with the dress. The Italians maybe didn't normally chat up their own countrywomen in the street. They were more interested in the foreigners. So much for wanting to look like a native!

Despite this fiasco I had the dress on again in the morning, for our last half day before catching the train to Munich and Ostend at 2.30pm. During our spare time we were once again nosing round the shops but I was now short of Italian money for last minute spending. However, I found some rather obscure Scots pound notes tucked into a corner of my wallet so I took them into a bank to get exchange. Well what a performance that was. The bank clerk looked suspiciously at my Austrian dress and my grubby Scots pound notes before hefting down a large volume of the world's paper money and leafing through it. Meanwhile a large queue formed behind me, all tutting in impatience and looking curiously at my attire, while listening to my stilted conversation with the bank clerk in an effort to get some small change. I began to wish the dress was in my pack at the hostel, or better still, in the shop where I'd been naive enough to buy it!

During all this kerfuffle at the bank I lost track of my companions, so I did a quick tour of the shops on my own before returning to the hostel to pick up my pack. There I found everyone ready to depart for the station and demanding to know where I'd been all morning, so I had to do a double quick change out my dress and catch them up. When we arrived at the station, where the club boys were now also assembled, we still had ten minutes before the train arrived, during which interval Jane and Susie were trying to fill a water bottle from a drinking fountain and getting more water on themselves than into the bottle.

The train journey to Munich was not particularly notable, except that a rail employee tried to turf us off at Innsbruck saying we had the wrong tickets. Ronnie argued the point with him and refused to budge so he stamped off red faced, while we sat on and eventually trundled across the border into Germany. For some reason at that time Austria was the most difficult country to get through, with constant security, customs checks and a military presence in the Brenner Pass.

The overnight train that took us from Munich to Ostend was packed solid and another party were sitting in our booked seats refusing to move, because they declared the seats were theirs. The crew seemed to be unable to sort out the debacle which left us sitting on our packs in the corridor, or trying to sleep on the floor!

When I returned to Pitlochry things seemed very dull after all our adventures, but I put on my Austrian dress and made ready to go down to the shops in it, at which point my mother said, "You look like a hotel waitress in that outfit," while a friend of hers said "Is that a Dutch costume?" So my beautiful Alpine dress was winning no points for approval anywhere. In Italy I hadn't fitted in and in Scotland it was being regarded as fancy dress! Sadly I packed it away in a drawer. In years to come I took it out and dismantled it, making it into a skirt, trimmed with lace and using strips from the apron to add a contrasting layer. Although I didn't wear it very often it's still in my chest of drawers fifty years later. Sometimes I take it out and admire the Austrian print design thinking, I could convert this into a couple of cushion covers!

After that first visit to the Alps I had Glasgow and the Langside Club to look forward to at the end of August and in two years time I would return to the Dolomites with my boyfriend. I really had no time to mourn the catastrophe of the Austrian dress!

# PART 3: GLASGOW & THE LANGSIDE 1965-67

# 1

# TEACHING IN GLASGOW &
# SCHOOL CHILDREN'S OUTING

It was the summer of 1965, when after my exhilarating holiday in the Dolomites with the Langside, I was to be experiencing a new beginning in Glasgow, both in teaching and living in digs – not to mention the real reason for the move being to climb with the Langside. After securing a job my next priority was digs and in this respect I travelled down to Glasgow to review the situation a couple of weeks before the schools restarted at the end of August.

Digs were plentiful in the west end of the city, which was also a popular area for students, but they varied considerably in price, décor, respectability and what they provided. They were almost exclusively in sandstone tenement properties, several flights of stairs up, and after inspecting a few, trying not to look too immature and gullible, I settled for one in Southpark Avenue. The room cost £2 per week, situated in a second floor flat with accommodation for six in single and double rooms, including communal use of kitchen and bathroom, with the cost being relative for fifty years ago! Having paid the deposit and crossed it off my 'to-do' list, I went back to Pitlochry to look out bed linen, towels and a suitable wardrobe of teaching, socializing and mountaineering apparel. It was a somewhat devious way of getting what I wanted out of life, which of course was climbing hills with like minded companions, but I was soon to question the prudence of this decision.

The next hurdle was my new city school. I'd already spent two years doing my probationary teaching practice in the Royal School of Dunkeld in Perthshire, where the children were mild mannered and polite, the headmaster supportive and the rural view out the window aesthetically pleasing. But all this was about to change in the kind of way I could never have envisaged, despite brief experiences during my teaching practice in Glasgow schools during college training.

The biggest mistake I made was in not investigating the school I had been allocated and the area in which it was situated, which led to the worst episode of my teaching career. The only thing I had been told was that it was in an inner city redevelopment area and not having much experience of Glasgow outside the closeted walls of the college campus and its environs on the outskirts of the city, I had no idea what a redevelopment area entailed. I thought perhaps it related to a new school building and housing schemes with green belts in between! Nothing could have been further from the truth. The school was an old grubby, square blocked, sandstone building, surrounded by stern, high, iron railings, enclosing a concrete playground, while nearby noisy demolition work was in progress regarding rows of smoke and industrial blackened, run down tenements, accompanied by volumes of dust and piles of rubble. A few shops opposite the school remained standing and in business, while in some already cleared wasteland areas, scruffily clad children poked about dirty puddles with broken sticks and metal bars, under a leaden grey sky and drizzling rain. A depressing aura hovered over the scene, conjuring up images of a post war zone and I had a sinking feeling of impending doom as I hurried in the school gates and entered the gloomy building.

Immediately I was aware of a smell compounded of sweat, BO and leaking lavatories, overlaid with cheap floor polish and a veneer of disinfectant. I wanted to turn around and run fast in the direction of the Education Office, to tell the authorities this had all been a big mistake. I really didn't want a job in Glasgow at all! But something made me climb the stairs and search for the staffroom.

When I opened the door I saw a group of young women, some in deep discussion and others scrutinising a notice board. I sidled over to the board for a look and found my name on a sheet of paper with the class I had been allocated. I digested the information and turned to the other members of staff to find out more about the establishment, but no one could enlighten me. They all seemed to be new comers like myself, except for one who was older and sat apart from the others, raking in a briefcase of paperwork. I had a sinking feeling of impending doom. Then a bell rang, long and shrill. The older woman got up, snapped her briefcase shut and told us to go to our classrooms. Was this it? No welcoming introduction?

There were about forty children in my class, aged around nine. They sat in regimental rows, facing the teacher's desk and the black board and they were staring at me sulkily, nudging and sniggering, sizing me up. I'd have to take charge quickly, so I opened my desk lid and took out the class register, calling out their names and ticking them off one by one, before looking for jotters to get them busy writing about their summer holidays and their families. What I hadn't realised was that such topics were inadvisable for inner city sixties youngsters, many of whom didn't go on a summer holiday and their families could be complicated with second or third marriages. I soon had a hand up asking if mother's new boyfriend who stayed over at weekends was actually a family member, which put me in a quandary!

To save time in the jotter distribution I put a pile on each front desk, telling them to pass the rest back, but this was another mistake as they were thrown back like net balls in a team race, some landing on the floor and others in the wrong row. 'Stop that!' I said, raising my voice, but they were already giggling and looking at me cheekily beneath furrowed brows, gauging my reaction. When I asked them politely to start by drawing me a picture of their family and pets it started a barrage of - 'I hav'nae got a pet', 'I hav'nae got a pencil – mine's broken - mine's blunt', or 'Please Miss - Jimmy's pinched mine', followed by a wrestling match on the floor. Pencils were supplied by the education authority and I had presumed they had one in their desk from the previous year, but this didn't seem to be the case. I searched frantically in the classroom cupboards for the authority's supplies, while noisy issues escalated behind me, with several individuals now out their seats. I repeatedly shouted at them to behave, despite the golden rule we'd learned at college, that a noisy teacher made a noisy class! My upbringing in private girls' schools in London and at Morrison's Academy had not prepared me for this, never mind the small country class in Dunkeld I'd recently left behind. I began to wish I'd stayed there!

The morning was a chaotic muddle through, until thankfully the strident bell sounded for break, when I hurried for respite in the staffroom and a cup of coffee. Some of the staff seemed to be used to the situation and were better prepared to deal with it, but another group were bitterly complaining. I gravitated towards this group and added my pennyworth of frustration to the discussion, then the door opened and the head teacher strode in. If we approached her for advice she made it plain that it was up to us to manage the classes we'd been allocated. Most of her time was spent in the head teacher's office with the door shut and when pressed for help her answer was always the same, 'Belt them. You'll find a belt in the desk.'

I was horrified. 'Belt them!?' Was this what inner city teaching was all about? I'd vaguely become aware during college teaching practice that the belt was the ultimate deterrent to bad behaviour, but I'd never envisaged myself resorting to such measures.

I found the belt at the bottom of my desk. It was a heavy leather tawse with two flails. I flinched and dropped it back into the desk like it was some nasty disagreeable insect, covering it with paperwork. I'd come to the city to meet climbers and explore the mountains of the west, not to wallop little kids. There must be some other way?

Things took a turn for the worse just before lunch when the window cleaners arrived with pails of water, step ladders, glass wipers and chamois cloths. The children's already unruly behaviour escalated with their appearance, as they called out cheeky remarks and pinged fragments of rubber at the windows and the backsides of the men, propelled from elastic bands.

My efforts to shut them up and bring back a measure of control failed miserably. I threatened them with lines, staying in at break, extra work or reporting them to a higher authority, without any expectations of what that might achieve – if anything? But I didn't mention the belt.

When the window cleaners left I heaved a sigh of relief, but ten minutes later they were back, this time on the outside, which led to more flying missiles directed at the glass, imitations of the washing action and rude signs.

Lunch time for a whole hour was a prize beyond belief, but I'd elected to have a school dinner first which I'd thought would save me cooking at night in the digs. Well it didn't! I only had one school dinner in that establishment. The racket in the dining hall echoing off hard, shiny surfaces was horrendous, accompanied by the odour of fat and overcooked vegetables emanating from the kitchen, while some of the children ate standing up and others were doing battle with the cutlery, trying to poke their neighbour's eye out with a fork! After that experience I decided to take a packed lunch and supplement it with a banana from the green grocer's across the road. The first time I asked for one banana some local women in the shop turned round with a sneer, muttering, 'Did you hear that? She only wants ONE banana?" From that day on I became known as 'Miss Snooty one banana,' although the shop assistant was actually a jovial man and always handed me one banana when he saw me coming in the door. I had the feeling that the locals were not used to the teaching profession gracing their local shops and the sight of my smart skirt, nylons and shiny high heels had upset them!

There were only two days before relief at the weekend, but next Monday I knew there was a whole week to survive. The younger staff were actually quite entertaining. We held frequent discussions concerning other jobs we might be able to tackle to escape from our present circumstances - and to temporarily liven things up a portable wind-up gramophone and vinyl records were brought in to provide distracting music at lunch time. Some jived on the threadbare carpet, while others started up a card school with games of knock out whist. Others hastily corrected jotters to save taking them home. There wasn't much preparation for lessons in those days, as text books were rigidly followed and there were answer books in the cupboard. Records of work accomplished each week were stringently kept and inspected.

I soldiered on in the establishment for several weeks, despite the children's impudent behaviour and a few unwelcome appearances at the classroom door, when irate, unshaven, sloppily clad parents presented themselves, complaining and threatening me if I had reprimanded their child for unruly misdemeanours. Despite this I gradually felt I was achieving a slight improvement in the general situation without resorting to the belt, as I had sussed out the things that grabbed their attention, one of which was singing, with my guitar being particularly appreciated. Glasgow kids loved to sing, but we couldn't sing all day. They also liked art and had a blast with self-expression when I showed them how to do rag paintings, producing some stunning results. The three R's however, only seemed to incite rebellion, with one lad shouting, "Please Miss, you don't need qualifications to be a dustbin emptier!" What hope was there for them if that was the height of their ambition?

I lasted eight weeks there, but the final crowning glory was not the horrendous behaviour or threatening parents. It was the fleas! There was a complete plague of them in the building and they all seemed keen to make in my direction. It wasn't long before I was covered in itchy bites. They were spreading up my legs, ending up as heads of pus that broke and wept down my nylons, so that I achieved little sleep at night as I spent so much time scratching. It was time to do something about my situation. I was living for the weekends and dreading the weeks. At night in the digs I would ruminate about a means of escape and it was often the chief topic of staffroom discussions.

One alternative discussed was 'Voluntary Service Overseas' (VSO), which had been talked about during my college years. Some people loved it as it was an opportunity to see the world, and several students had obtained forms. The paperwork gave a list of possible places where you could be sent and you could state preferences, but there was no guarantee that you would get anything near to your choice. I'd seen the Falkland Islands in the list, which was next door to Antarctica and obviously very attractive to me, being the nearest that a girl could get to the south polar regions at that time. However, I quickly realised that I was more likely to be offered a hot, sweaty region in the tropics, with no refusal being allowed once the application was dispatched. I'd decided not to take the risk!

Now, when the subject was mentioned again in the staffroom I declined to get involved, because I had another plan that might be more flexible. The first Glasgow boyfriend that I'd cultivated was a handsome, amorous lad that I'd met on a weekend in Glencoe. He was more of a weekender than a hill walker, but he listened to my complaints about the unsatisfactory school, before making an enticing suggestion. Along with another couple he said we could get a large van, give up our jobs and go travelling on the continent. He made it sound amazing, but alarm bells started to pop up regarding the domestic arrangements! In this respect I withdrew from 'man with van on the continent' and hatched up a simpler escape, which I implemented at the end of my eighth week in Glasgow. I simply walked out the door of the school on Friday afternoon without any intention of returning!

I hurried down to Queen Street Station with a suitcase and caught an evening train to Pitlochry, and 'No' I was not running home to mother. I had plan number three, which was to drop off luggage at home before hitching on north to the sanctuary of the Highlands and getting myself a job as a hotel waitress. I'd done waitressing jobs in my student holidays. Despite the inferior pay, I liked the work, could live in, meet a variety of people and have a laugh – and best of all de-stress. The parents wouldn't be pleased, that was for sure, so I spent the journey rehearsing points for

94

the battle I knew was going to ensue as soon as I walked in the door.

After weeks of subdued anger this was about to be released and without preamble it hit the ceiling as I stepped inside, describing the hell on earth I had been forced to put up with teaching in Glasgow and throwing it back at them how surprised I was that they should want their daughter to be working in such a place. I think my mother was quite shocked, but my father said, "You can't just walk out! You'll have to discuss the position with the director and see if anything can be done about the situation."

Angry as I was, I knew he had a point. I went upstairs to my room and taking out a notepad and pen, I filled several sheets with my complaints. Leaving no stone unturned I described the situation from hell that had evolved, the unruly, impudent behaviour, the threatening parents, the lack of co-operation from senior officers and most of all the infestations of fleas.

I knew that a month's notice was expected before withdrawing from a post and to be considered for a transfer, so I took a chance and pointed out that I would complete this stipulation with Glasgow Education Authority in another school, then I pushed the sheets into an envelope, stamped and addressed it and went out in the dark to drop it into the nearest post box before I could change my mind. I had not suddenly shelved the waitressing alternative, but I was well aware of the drop in wages it would entail, never mind the three years I had wasted getting my certificate of education for teaching in primary schools in the first place.

"It's done," I announced flatly to my parents.

"I hope you were polite," my father answered with a worried frown.

"Chillingly so," I said, before going upstairs again to write another epistle, to a hill climbing girl friend I'd met in the city, who worked as a secretary in the offices of the Director of Education in Bath Street!

It was Monday afternoon before I boarded the train back to Glasgow to face the wrath of the city's education department. On Tuesday morning

I presented myself at the appointed office and was told the Director was out, investigating my complaints. This was a bad sign and one which I should have anticipated. Of course he was going to investigate and the head teacher would undoubtedly have a golden opportunity to deny everything, turn the tables around and ground me forcefully into the mire. The director would then be in a quandary. I was an underling with few rights. If he took my side, reprimanded her and she left, he might have difficulty getting a willing replacement for the position. He would play safe I was sure. I was more expendable than she was.

In due course he returned to the office where I waited with baited breath. He looked at me, frowning under furrowed brows, so that I knew my assumptions had been correct. "So," he said, with an edge to his voice. "It seems you didn't ask for sufficient advice."

"But I did," I began, suddenly feeling intimidated in front of this important man in his immaculate suit. There was a brief silence before he continued, changing tack.

"So you want another position? I only have one other primary school vacancy at the moment. It's in Castlemilk." He named the school and asked if I was agreeable.

I was gobsmacked as I stood there nervously in front of him. He'd just thrown me a lifeline. He'd offered me another school without further questions or recrimination. Castlemilk conjured up a rather unsavoury option, but before I could say anything he continued with the ghost of a smile. "It's a brand new school on the outer edge of Castlemilk, with a grand view over the city. A member of staff there is going off on maternity leave tomorrow. Will you take her class?"

It was another question and he was waiting for an answer.

"I'll go," I said. "Thank you." There was no alternative and I knew I should try again.

"Good luck," he said as I shut the door with a sigh of relief.

Luckily I hadn't given up my digs. I went to the Ceylon Tea Centre for a snack before catching the bus back to Southpark Avenue, but I hadn't gone far when I had a nasty thought. I'd left all my project books from college on the Romans and the Vikings, which were valuable teaching aids, in my desk at the school I'd just fled. I'd put a great deal of work into those books and I had to get them back.

With this in mind I jumped off the bus at the next stop and walked back towards the inner city. It wasn't quite time for school dismissal and I couldn't risk bumping into the head teacher, so I contrived a plan. The old green grocer's shop opposite the school gates was the place. I dashed in the door, while the good natured owner proffered me my one banana. "Not today thank you," I said. "I need a favour from you."

I thought quickly. "I'm playing a trick on someone. Can I hide for a few minutes behind your orange boxes?" He chuckled and nodded, before moving away to attend to another customer.

I kept my eye to the crack between two boxes, watching for the head teacher to leave the premises before scooting across to the front door. Being a creature of habit, she was always sharp in leaving, and this afternoon was no exception as I watched her striding towards the gate and hurrying up the road, before rounding the corner out of sight.

"Thanks," I called to the genial shop keeper. He wasn't to know he'd never see me again.

I ran across the road and dived into the school, taking the staircase at a gallop as I made for my old classroom. On my way I passed two cleaners with buckets and mops, but I scurried past them and dived into my room, which fortunately was empty. I was praying that the books were still there and thankfully they were. Sweeping them into my bag with relief, I turned without another glance and hurried out the building. But in the front hall I met the janitor. "Well hullo there, what's going on?" he called, looking for gossip.

"I'm sorry, but I'm leaving," I muttered under my breath. It wasn't his fault people left.

"No one ever stays long," he said ruefully.

"Sorry," I mumbled again. Then I was gone, racing up the road to the bus stop. I supposed I was a failure. Should I have tried harder? Well it was too late now. I'd make a fresh start in Castlemilk. The thought did not inspire me with much enthusiasm.

I'd been told it was a long journey out to the heights of Castlemilk on the outskirts of the city so I set my alarm for 7 o'clock. Despite this I had a scramble to get ready and didn't have time for breakfast, so I threw bread, butter, marmalade and a knife into a paper bag in my brief case before hurrying out the door. I caught the underground to St Enoch, where I had to change into a double-decker bus. All the buses coming in to St Enoch at that time were packed, but the ones going back out were almost empty. I climbed up to the top deck and sat in the back seat, waiting till we'd cleared the centre of the city before I took out my breakfast. I was about to enjoy it, using a box lid as a plate, when the young conductor appeared at the top of the stair, casting wistful eyes in my direction, so we shared the spoils as the empty bus rattled along, threading the endless bland, grey streets towards Castlemilk.

It kept me from worrying about the school, but as we approached the terminus I knew it was time to face the music. Had the Director of Education told my new head master about my past behaviour? I couldn't be sure as I nervously knocked on the door of his office. One thing was certain. It was definitely a new building and the Director had been right about the view from the school gates across to the distant Campsie Hills.

A kindly middle aged man opened the door and immediately invited me inside, offering a cup of tea. Well that was a good start. In due course he said he'd introduce me to my class, where I could spend the day shadowing the present teacher who would be leaving at the end of the afternoon.

As soon as he opened the classroom door I had another surprise. "Nancy!" I blurted, while she ran forward to greet me effusively. The head teacher stepped back bemused. "Do you two know each other?" he said.

Nancy had been the Jordanhill student who befriended me on my first skiing course at Glenmore Lodge in the Cairngorms in 1959, but over the past six years we had lost touch. At once I felt at home and I knew that although things might not be easy, they would certainly be a whole lot better than what I'd left behind.

Nancy had the class well organised so it was relatively easy to step into her shoes and keep the ball rolling. School dinners were also excellent, the dining hall well supervised and staff served separately at a table on the platform.

The drawbacks were the distance I had to travel to get there and to a certain extent, the staff, who were less charismatic than those I had left behind. They were older than I was, married with families and set in their ways. There would be no jigging on the carpet and card schools here and they were only mildly amused when I regaled them with tales of my bothy weekends in Glencoe on a Monday morning! I tolerated the morning break chit chat mostly concerning shop, but at lunch time I took my class to the gymnasium to play non-stop cricket. In my previous work place it had been the staff who cheered me up, but here it was the children.

In this respect I decided to start up the Saturday hill walking days I'd done as a student with some of my teaching practice kids. It had initially been under the scheme 'Adventure on your Doorstep' aimed at introducing city children to the countryside, but I took it a step further and invited a group from my class to the hills beside Loch Lomond. I had a signed note of consent from the parents whose children were involved which was all that was required in those days. There was great enthusiasm for these excursions which I initiated about once a month, as most of the kids had never climbed a hill before or even seen Loch Lomond. Initially we went to Balloch, travelling on a double-decker bus from Glasgow, singing all the way, with often other passengers and the conductor joining in. 'Ye canna shove yer grannie aff a bus,' being the favourite.

I tried to make sure that the children were suitably clad for these expeditions, but many of them didn't have windproof jackets or stout shoes. On one occasion a young lassie turned up with flimsy sandals, but when I pointed out the shortcomings of such footwear for the terrain involved she explained soulfully that she only had one pair of shoes. I was just beginning to realise how poor some of these children were and I kicked myself for passing the remark in the first place, covering it up with - "Don't worry. It's a fine day so it won't be too muddy. You'll be OK."

I never excluded the poorest children on the walks, because they were the ones with least opportunity to experience the mountains, and they were often the most grateful, thanking me profusely and saying they would always remember their wonderful day in the country. As a change from Balloch and Ben Bowie on the banks of Loch Lomond, we also went to Balmaha where we climbed Conic Hill, and sometimes we were really adventurous and hired a rowing boat to go out to Inchcailloch Island. It was a real Treasure Island experience for them. We walked across the island through verdant green woodlands and tall flowering plants. then we picnicked on a wide sandy bay at the far side before gathering souvenirs to take home - unusual stones and large leaves. On one occasion some of the girls collected giant rhubarb like leaves in Balmaha, which they were using as parasols, then when the bus arrived to take them back to Glasgow they wanted to take the leaves aboard, which was vetoed by the conductor!

At the end of the school year I applied for another position in a school which involved less travelling. This undoubtedly was going to take me back closer to the inner city, but I thoroughly investigated all vacant opportunities first, settling on one in Parkhead. It was an old style building and my class were younger, but the head master was efficient and I had more in common with the staff. Several were my age, staying in digs in the west end and as one conveniently had a car she volunteered to transport three of us to work every day in exchange for petrol money, which was bliss.

I stayed two years at Parkhead and soon had the children on Saturday outings to the country again, with mixed expeditions to Loch Lomond and the Campsies. I have many enduring memories of that school, including the time one of the staff put on a blond wig, knocked at the head teacher's door and pretended to be a senior officer from the education office who had arrived to carry out an inspection! On another occasion the whole school marched through the streets in a crocodile to attend an Easter service in a local church, where one of the hymns was 'Lord of the Dance'. The children quickly caught on to the catchy tune and when we left they sang and danced all the way back to the school, drawing much attention to themselves from passers by!

My children's expeditions gradually became more ambitious, and for older primary school boys they included a trip across Loch Lomond from Balloch to Rowardennan in the 'Maid of the Loch' paddle steamer, followed by an ascent of Ben Lomond which was a substantial achievement for them. Our most technically difficult expedition was an ascent of the Cobbler at Arrochar, climbing through the eye of the Cobbler's needle on exposed rock to access the summit. I kept them well secured on a top rope for this final section, which was a thrilling and memorable experience.

Only twice did I have any bother with a group I took to the mountains and on the first occasion it was another expedition to Arrochar with the aim of climbing the Cobbler, but when we alighted from the bus it was raining and the mist was down on the tops. We decided to walk along the shore instead looking for specimens washed up by the sea, but the boys were more interested in an old boat we came upon, tethered to a post. Before I could stop them they had clambered aboard and disappeared down a hatch. When they reappeared they were each wearing a life jacket they had found below.

"Put those back right now," I said in alarm. "They're someone else's property."

The lifejackets were eventually and grudgingly restored below and we carried on along the shore, then I was aware of giggling behind me. When

I turned round one of the boys had a life jacket stuffed up his jumper! He was frog marched back to the boat to return it, protesting strongly. I have to say though, that on this occasion the boys were not from my regular class. They were older boys from primary seven who had shown interest in an outing.

Concerning rock climbing I took small groups of younger lads to the Whangie on several occasions. This was a cliff in the Kilpatrick hills used by Glasgow climbers for practising technique on short routes in an evening. There were many easy routes as well, which I knew would give them a thrill and these excursions were very successful. Other adult climbers there at the time often gave me a hand which was helpful and allowed us to achieve more challenging ascents.

My other incident on an outing occurred during my one and only expedition to Edinburgh to climb Arthur's Seat. We had decided to extend the day with a walk up the Royal Mile to have a look at the castle, which most of them had never seen - and this was where disaster struck. During the walk up to the castle gates some of them lagged behind. There were numerous distractions along the Royal Mile and I noticed that some of the boys were loitering at the window of an antique shop, giggling and laughing. Then I suddenly realised what they had been doing, for the window was smeared in mouldy banana from someone's piece box. I was mortified. "Get that off there right now!" I said in alarm, while passers by muttered, 'Disgraceful!' I sought to accelerate the cleaning before the shop owner came on the scene, and in this respect I soaked a handkerchief in a nearby puddle to scrub at the sticky smears. Then when a policeman on the beat appeared, we all guiltily scarpered.

My last school in the Central Belt was out at Johnstone where I transferred to after John and I married and had our own flat in Mount Florida. The constant pressure of the urban environment was becoming depressing but the school in Johnstone, which came under Renfrewshire Education Authority, was situated on the edge of the Glennifer Braes. Even the long journey to get there on two commuter trains was worth it for a brief sniff of the countryside.

The school children came from more affluent homes and when I organised expeditions to the hills they turned up with good quality equipment, waterproof jackets and boots. In one way this wasn't quite as rewarding as taking out the poorer children, but in another it enabled me to tackle more ambitious projects. My husband was now involved to help so we started a club for the most interested youngsters. We held day trips to Glencoe to climb the Pap in early winter snow and we had a weekend expedition to Fort William by train to climb Ben Nevis, with an overnight stay in a caravan in the glen below.

In five years we had progressed from Ben Bowie at Balloch to Scotland's highest mountain, while at the same time I was weekending with the Langside and revelling in the Glencoe dosses.

# 2

# THE CLUB AND GLENCOE DOSSES

With my reason for returning to Glasgow being the Langside Mountaineering Training Centre most of my free time was spent connected to it. Monday evenings were occupied with tourist German classes in an endeavour to be able to communicate with people next time I went to the Alps, Tuesday was my folk club night to increase my repertoire of songs for weekend entertainment in Glencoe, Wednesday was the Langside club and Thursday was reserved for essential washing, packing and preparation for the weekend.

Wednesday was the highlight of the week. Meetings were held in a basement apartment at Langside College where we had talks, slide shows, knot tying practice, map and compass work and discussion on forthcoming weekends, before going over to the gym where a practice wall for rock climbing had been installed, ahead of its time for the mid sixties. It was riveting stuff with chimneys, mantle shelves, missing and protruding bricks and half bricks, and rings in the wall and ceiling for abseiling and belaying. Nowadays there are very sophisticated indoor climbing walls in leisure and training centres and there are outdoor climbing facilities and via ferratas in disused quarries throughout the country. At the Langside in the sixties it was a huge novelty to have access to this early artificial climbing wall and afterwards there was fitness training and swimming in the college pool. Finally there was the late night café in Battlefield Road where members repaired to plan the weekend, organise lifts, hitchhiking partners and climbing mates. At one time a monthly bus was hired for club weekends, but that had more or less stopped when I joined, apart from one at New Year.

Surprisingly all the hitchers seemed to make it on Friday nights from Balloch. They had a strict protocol for this activity on the Glencoe route.

All members taking part queued behind a garage on the opposite side of the road from the hitching spot on the outskirts of Balloch, apart from one person, the designated hitcher. When a vehicle stopped he would ask the driver how many he could take and if it was three he would hold up three fingers to the boys hiding in the shadows by the garage. I used to think this was a bit cheeky, but that was the rule.

I'd already had my fingers rapped for inadvertently transgressing the rules in this spot before I joined the club. I'd arrived in Glasgow a couple of weeks before the club resumed it's regular winter session and at my digs I'd met a French girl, Claude, who was keen to do some walking in Scotland. We'd organised a weekend at Ardgarten Youth Hostel and planned to climb the Cobbler just beyond Arrochar. With this in mind we set off on Friday night to get a local train to Balloch, from where we were going to hitch and having arrived at the designated spot on the main road north, we were unaware that a group of Glasgow lads who regularly went to Glencoe throughout the year were skulking behind the garage opposite. Only one person was visible hitching so we stood a few yards along from him and when a vehicle appeared I put out my thumb. The car whizzed past without stopping, but a tornado suddenly appeared beside us, when the other guy with his thumb out marched over and reprimanded us for our behaviour, pointing out that there was a queue across the road to take part, who were suddenly making their presence felt! I viewed the shadowy line of aggrieved figures with distaste and shouldering my pack I said, "Well if that's the case we'll walk on. There's no law about that!" Without a backward glance we marched off round the corner and got a lift immediately, leaving the large queue and their earmarked hitcher fuming!

Round about the time I joined the Langside they had acquired a doss in Glencoe which they had decided would be a good base, preferable to camping, especially in winter and wet weather and would save carrying cumbersome gear. The doss room was within a group of barns on the roadside, at the south end of Glencoe in the Lagangarbh area, not too far from Kingshouse Hotel and extremely convenient for Buachaille Etive Mor with its grandiose, wide ranging rock climbing opportunities.

Members of the Langside were mostly tradesmen with skills in joinery, plumbing, electrical work, brick laying, painting and decorating, so it wasn't long before the doss house floor was cemented, a wood burning stove installed and an Alpine sleeping shelf erected under the rafters, accessed by a ladder. Incidentally what I used to call a bothy in the Cairngorms seemed to be a doss in Glencoe, although according to the dictionary a bothy is a hut used for temporary shelter, while a doss refers to a cheap lodging house for homeless people. Well I suppose we were homeless at the weekend! 'Doss' can also sum up any kind of makeshift shelter, as can a howff.

Our particular doss exuded character and warmth from the stove, paraffin lamps, candles and gently hissing primus stoves, while ice axes, belay lengths, ropes and karabiners hung from pegs on the wall. However, 'mod cons' were decidedly lacking. Water was fetched from convenient streams and a call to the loo entailed a visit to the woods across the road! The doss became my perfect weekend retreat. It was suffused in magical charm, resounding with yarns, music, banter and the clink of mountaineering ironmongery, while shadows flickered round the walls, mixed with the odour of wood smoke, paraffin, candle grease, fried burgers and onions. We were a family that I felt I belonged to and was accepted by, despite most of them being men. Home had never been like this. I couldn't wait to open the door on Friday night.

We all had a common aim, escaping from Glasgow into the wilds of Glencoe, where the sheer rock walls and high mountain ridges provided a playground for ambition and achievement. At the same time I couldn't help thinking that my particular escape was not so much from the drudgery and claustrophobia of industrial Glasgow as it was from something entirely different - a strict Victorian childhood!

Another club called the Eilde had a doss next door, while the Scottish Mountaineering Club had the cottage referred to as Lagangarth nearby and across the river was Jacksonville owned by the illustrious Creag Dhu. Members of all these organisations and various others met in Kingshouse Hotel on Saturday nights or at the Glencoe village hall dances. Although I used the Langside doss and sometimes climbed and walked with club members, I didn't form a personal relationship with any of them, mainly because most of them were younger that I was. They were lads not many years out of school, whereas I had already left college and had a professional job, not that being professional had anything to do with it, but I tended to climb with older blokes from other clubs who also hung around Glencoe. Some of these were from the Glasgow University (GUM) Club and others were from the Starav, a club which had been formed from ex-Langside members. I met a guy from the Starav Club in the Glencoe village dance hall one Saturday night and we had a huge laugh when I discovered that he was the arrogant hitcher who had chastised me for my behaviour at the Balloch hitching spot ten months previous! After this night in Glencoe I recorded my second meeting with John in my 1966 diary of the period as 'got landed with John Quinn!'

Eighteen months later when we were married in Fishers Hotel in Pitlochry he described the incident at the Balloch hitching spot and the Glencoe dance hall in his after dinner speech, which brought the house down with the climbing fraternity present!

Meanwhile my increasing association with John led to shifting my Glencoe doss to the other end of the glen, to the Starav club premises which was on the back road to Glencoe village, near the youth hostel and Clachaig Hotel. John had been one of the founder members of the Starav who were all men. They had secured the use of a barn on a local farm owned by Sorley McCall in exchange for work done on the farm, including fencing jobs, plumbing work at the farm house, helping at the sheep gathering and on days to the mart on the west coast. I'm not sure who got the bigger part of the bargain there as the barn doss was nothing like the Langside premises. It was decidedly filthy I have to say, still with cobbled floor inset with dung in some places and no sleeping shelf.

Instead it had old rickety bedsteads with well worn mattresses to throw sleeping bags on, but there was the bonus of a cold water tap outside the door. Another attribute was the possibility of sneaking into the farm bunkhouse nearby and using their toilet facilities!

Fortunately the barn situation didn't last long, because they had permission to build a wooden hut on the farm ground. Old sleepers were procured for the floor, and a firm that John had worked for in Glasgow donated three wooden huts that were surplus to their requirements and could be converted into one. The work was largely carried out by John's elder brother who was a joiner, with help from the other members of the club at weekends, and the result was a commodious, cosy doss with typical Alpine sleeping shelf, a stove, wooden table and bench, pegs for equipment and a hut log book to record climbs. Still missing was electric light and running water, although the tap was nearby and a disconnected WC pedestal reposed in a corner cupboard. Maybe one day we wouldn't have to sneak down to the bunkhouse! The Starav doss was a lot handier for the pub at Clachaig, also the dance hall in Glencoe village and climbs at the top end of the glen.

My weekending in Glencoe lasted for about two years, sharply contrasting with my week's teaching in city schools and won me no favours in school staffroom Monday morning chat, where other members of staff had no idea why anyone would want to do that kind of thing, far less enjoy it!

# 3

# CLIMBING DAYS & WEEKENDS FROM GLASGOW

## THE MAMORES

During my first two years back in Glasgow I climbed with a variety of people and clubs, including Langside members, the Glasgow University Mountaineering Club (GUM Club), which Jane had joined and the Starav Club, as well as individuals. A number of days stood out for various reasons, but one of the most memorable took place in the Mamores at the head of Glen Nevis, which was about as far as we ventured for a weekend.

It was March sixty-six when I joined a group from the GUM club for weekend at Steall Hut, in the vicinity of the Mamores. We'd arrived in Glen Nevis in darkness, late on Friday night and had a strenuous scramble through Steall Gorge to reach the hut. Clambering over giant boulders in the pass, laden with gear, the river thrashing and boiling beside us and only our head torches lighting up the Stygian dark was quite an operation, and of course there was a sting in the tail, for we had to cross the Water of Nevis on a dicey wire bridge to reach the hut. I also had my guitar which I seldom went without, although on this particular occasion I could have seen it far enough! The bridge was a balancing act with a narrow wire below and two swinging hand rails above, while the river made intimidating noise underneath.

The following day the weather was stunning and our Mamore traverse turned into an epic with incredible panoramic views to rival the Swiss Alps. Jim and I teamed up and climbed six peaks that day as we made our way along high ice encrusted ridges and snow covered tops, amongst which were Binnein Beag, Binnean Mor, Na Gruagaichean, An Garbhanach, Am Bodach and Sgurr a'Mhaim, part of which is known as the Ring of Steall and including the excitement of the Devil's Ridge, all made easier and safer due to the use of crampons. Darkness was falling as we finally descended from the ridge in torch light to our overnight quarters, replete with a warm glow of achievement, followed by an evening of good craic, folk singing and games of liar dice around the fire. Liar dice was the bothy game of the period, requiring only five dice and a certain amount of wit to catch the other players out. In fact we became so obsessed with it on that particular weekend that some of us played it all the way back to Glasgow in the back seat of the car!

## GLENCOE

In Glencoe one of the most iconic hills was Buachaille Etive Mor which lay in close proximity to the Langside doss at the southern entrance to the glen. It could be climbed by any number of severe and exposed rock routes, or by Curved Ridge, a moderate to difficult route that the serious rock climber would consider a scramble, or alternately by a stiff walking route up the back, so that the summit was not denied to the moderate walking enthusiast. The exposure on the face routes was nothing like that in the Dolomites, but any exposure can be intimidating and Curved Ridge, which I climbed several times was no exception. There were stances on it from which photographs could be taken to make it look a lot more awe inspiring and severe than it really was, and one such photograph that John took of me on the skyline was later dug out from the archives and liberally displayed in Badaguish Lodge that we hired in the Cairngorms for my 70th birthday!

As well as climbing in Glencoe, Langside members also spent time in Glen Etive and Glenorchy to the south. During my first months with the club it was the autumn hill padding season so I used this opportunity to polish off a few Munro's I had not done. I also took the opportunity to do some hill scrambling on my own as in the days of my youth in Crieff, taking in peaks that the club boys generally ignored, as not being seriously difficult enough to merit wasting a whole day of a precious weekend. In contrast to the Cairngorms there was not much of a walk in to the mountains bordering either side of the glen and the tops could be easily attained in a daily jaunt. The biggest attraction was the rock, and in winter there was ice, but there were also nasty unexpected surprises, because bad weather could be lethal and one such narrow escape that I was involved in occurred on Bidean.

## HURRICANE ON BIDEAN

The north side of the glen was dominated by the Aonach Eagach Ridge which I did twice from end to end, including the Pap, during my sojourns to Glencoe, but the opposite side of the road boasted not only the highest peak in the glen which was Bidean, but the most photographed on calendars and cards, this being Buachaille Etive Mor. I had already climbed Bidean with Anne, but during my involvement with the Starav club we chose to do a winter climb onto one of the ridges radiating from the summit. Four of us set out, although two had planned a different route to the one John and I had chosen, but as they couldn't locate it in the rather misty conditions prevailing in the corrie they joined forces with us.

We cramponed up a steep snow slope to the crest of the ridge with no problem, but suddenly as we surmounted the final section and clambered onto the open exposure of the ridge itself there was a big problem, for unbeknown to us a hurricane force wind was blasting over the ridge from the opposite side. The intention had been to make our descent towards the North west but we soon found this was impossible as it was facing into the teeth of the wind. Razor sharp ice chips were hurtling towards us, smacking against exposed skin, our trousers and anoraks, and preventing us from keeping our eyes open. It was all happening so quickly. One minute, everything had been calm, and now it was like hell on earth. All we could do was turn our backs on it and stagger in the opposite direction towards the summit of Bidean and an escape route on the far side - but suddenly the mist was down again as well. It was like pea soup. We became disorientated on the narrow ridges that stretched out from the summit like tentacles on an octopus, most of which plunged down to the corries below in almost vertical sweeps, or terminated abruptly in equally perpendicular buttresses. The ice chip onslaught was continually battering us from behind and it was becoming important to get off the ridge at the first possible minute, before we were blown off!

Tense arguments developed on a plan of action but fortunately we found the summit cairn and managed to re-orientate ourselves. It was proposed that we head for the Lost Valley which was the descent Anne and I had used in 1963, but locating it in the mist was not easy. Then it was suggested we drop down on the other side of the mountain where the terrain was less steep, but this was voided as the long walk out to get back to the doss might precipitate a mountain rescue attempt in respect of our late return. John at this point declared the Lost Valley was on our left and volunteered to abseil over the cornice fringing the ridge to see if this was correct. We held our breath during this operation, but he gave us the thumbs up so we heaved a sigh of relief and one by one we dropped over the edge where there was immediate shelter from the bombardment above.

As we descended we were only dimly aware of the roar continuing in the distance as we sheepishly hurried down to the valley floor, before making our way through the huge, jumbled boulders that disguised the entrance to the valley from below, aptly named 'Lost'. A narrow path led downhill from there, eventually arriving at the Meeting of the Three Waters and the Glencoe road. Needless to say this was not one of our more successful expeditions and the next two incidents described were even less so.

# ACCIDENTS DON'T ALWAYS HAPPEN
# ON THE HILL

This episode took place on a climbing weekend with the Langside, but it had nothing to do with mountaineering. It had to do with a motor car – a Shooting Brake design, popular in the period, which one of the club's instructors had borrowed for the trip. It was more commodious than the proverbial mini van and could take four comfortably along with gear behind. A camping trip had been organised in the Trossachs in October, where we would tackle short rock routes on Ben a'Ann, a popular hill with climbers and easily accessible from Glasgow. Three of us had accepted a lift in the Shooting Brake, myself and Roni, who features in my book on the Cairngorms were in the back and another lad was in front with the driver.

We had assembled on Friday night at a pub near St Enoch Station, this being in the era before drink driving laws and compulsory seat belts in cars. Time was getting on when we left and it was already dark, but we didn't have too far to go to reach the Trossachs. On clearing the city we headed for Aberfoyle, after which it was over the high and winding Duke's Pass to Loch Achray, where we were going to erect the club tents.

Ironically we were only about five minutes from our destination when disaster struck. It was drizzling rain and the pass was wet and slippery with piles of slushy autumn leaves lying near the verges. Suddenly I was aware of a large white, concrete, council litter bin illuminated in the headlights. It was straight in front of us as we sped crazily towards it, but with a last minute manic swerve our driver missed it and we careered across to the other side of the road. Then there was no road - only darkness. I felt my shoulders glancing off the roof of the car, then a thump – and suddenly we stopped! There was silence, and through a slight haze I heard water running. Where was that coming from?

"Get out the car!" shouted the driver - and simultaneously all the doors flew open and we stumbled out into about six inches of water!

Someone found a torch and shone it around. We were standing in a wide shallow river. There was no sign of the road. Above us on our right was a high embankment covered in heather and bracken, some of it squashed flat. It was rising at perhaps a forty-five degree angle, maybe more, and with a shock we realised we had descended this slope in one complete sideways roll. I'd been totally unaware of this at the time.

Fortunately we were all able to walk and reasonably intact, apart from shock and bruising, some of us more extensively so than others, with the front seat passenger having the most significant bruising to his back and ribs to show for the experience. "Get the gear and the tents out," the driver instructed, quickly taking charge of the situation. "We'll have to walk to the camping place."

During the fall the rear doors of the Shooting Brake had burst open and the tent poles were in the river, but the backpacks were still inside. We managed to rescue all essential gear and drag it up the slope to the road, after which we walked for a short distance until we found the flat camping area in the trees near the local hotel. We also found the others there who had arrived before us by different means. Our party were decidedly subdued. The driver announced he'd lost his wallet and all night I couldn't lie on my right side because my ribs hurt when I drew breath. I'd remarked earlier to no one in particular that my eggs I'd brought for breakfast were all broken, to which there had been a facetious reply, "You're lucky that's all that's broken!"

In the morning it was raining again so there was no talk of climbing. Our driver had to hitch into Aberfoyle to contact Breakdown Services to pull the car back up the embankment, and most of the rest of us spent the day in the pub playing a game of 'Pennypush' along one of the bar room tables.

The next day there were some rock routes tackled done on Ben a'Ann, but most of us who had been in the accident spectated. The car incidentally, and also surprisingly, was still operating after being returned to the road, but I took a lift back to Glasgow with someone else and the experience left me wary of cars and drivers for some time.

# AN UNEXPECTED VISITOR

The next incident had nothing to do with climbing or cars. It had to do with phobias, of which I had two – spiders and cows! It happened on the Cobbler, in the so called Arrochar Alps as described by Glasgow climbers. I'd gone there for a camping weekend with Jim, my boyfriend from the Mamores, along with a few other climbers from different clubs, and we'd set up camp in a sheltered green basin not far from the rock climbing area. It was good weather on the Saturday and everyone was out on the rock, pitting their wits against numerous routes of different standard. One of the climbs we tackled was a bit outwith my capabilities and I became gripped trying to make a move from a perpendicular corner onto the face, where there were few sizeable holds. My companion was irritated at the delay, while I became a trifle stressed, and when I eventually reached the top I told him I was finished climbing for the day and would see him later back at the tent!

"Fine," he said and marched off to join some of the lads planning another climb.

When I reached the tent I crawled inside, zipped the door shut and lay on top of my sleeping bag reading a book, but a short while later I heard footsteps outside the tent.

"Is that you back?" I shouted without opening the door.

There was no answer, apart from a few sniffs – then I heard clattering amongst our dirty breakfast dishes that we'd left under the flysheet.

"What are you doing?" I shouted again. "I was going to wash those dishes in the stream later."

There was still no answer. Sitting up inside the tent I called out in exasperation, "All right then Cross Patch. There's no need for the silent treatment just because I was stuck on that climb for a few minutes!"

The lack of an answer was infuriating, but there was another pronounced sniff and a loud snap as of something breaking. I stiffened. At this point I'd had enough and with a flourish I pulled up the zip on the door, only to be confronted with a large black hairy face and two fearsome horns! The startled animal with a piece of bacon dangling from its mouth backed away hastily as I struggled to pull back the zip with shaking hands. There had been no sign of the climbers.

Hardly daring to move I sat tight in my canvas shelter, trembling in shock and breathing heavily, but there was no more shuffling outside the tent. Half an hour later I heard human voices at last and dared to re-open the door, where I saw Jim amongst the group. He seemed to be in good form so I recounted my episode with the cow he said, "Oh they're just over there, a whole herd of them."

Looking to where he was pointing I caught sight of a dozen or so grazing not that far away and I cringed. "Don't worry," he said. "I'll soon shift them." Grabbing a sling and karabiner he whirled it around his head and dashed up the slope towards them screaming like a demented cowboy, while the startled animals suddenly took off at speed in the opposite direction.

After that I felt thoroughly ashamed, but I have to say I'm not keen to walk through a field of grazing cattle unless there is a good stout fence between us. Surprising how priorities and ambitions change. When I was a youngster of primary school age I wanted to keep a cow for a pet and despite intervening years of giving them a wide berth, I later developed a great affinity with Highland Cattle in Lairg!

# THE WHANGIE

A quick spin out of Glasgow in the evening took one into the Kilpatrick Hills on the road to Drymen where there were excellent cliff faces for climbing in a narrow defile called 'The Whangie'. They provided short practice rock climbs, good for learning technique and were accessed by walking for about a mile and a half round to the far side of a low grassy hill. The cliff was hidden from the road and was an incredible playground for Glasgow climbers short of time for going further afield. It even had its own guide book, put together with numbered drawings on several maps. Most climbs on either side of the defile were between twenty and forty feet long and were well used in the sixties before artificial walls became popular.

You didn't have to possess a car or resort to hitching to reach the Whangie either, as buses from Buchanan Street bus station in Glasgow passed the spot on the way to Drymen. I'd taken boys from my class to climb there as it was an exciting place for youngsters and quite safe as long as they were roped up, while I belayed them from the top.

Almost half a century after we used to climb at the Whangie, John and I were in the area of the Kilpatrick Hills in 2013 and we decided to stop in the Whangie car park and walk round to have a nostalgic look at the cliffs. We saw changes immediately, with the car park being about three times the size, and there were large graphic sign boards advertising the historical significance of the area, in addition to warnings about litter. The park was already busy with cars and camper vans and people were preparing to start walking on the path leading across the hill, along with assorted dogs, young children and extensive picnic supplies. "Goodness me – it's got busy out here," I said, "but I don't see much sign of climbing gear."

We followed behind a party of dog walkers and a couple with binoculars and cameras slung round their necks, who were conversing in a foreign language. Shortly we came upon another group of rather oversized individuals in shorts, who were relaxing on a grassy knoll, looking ahead at a distant and hazy view of Loch Lomond.

"Is that Loch Lomond?" inquired a drawly American accent as we passed by. "My – your country is so beautiful." We nodded and kept walking. The ordinary tourist never went to the Whangie fifty years ago, far less without a climbing rope. We began to wonder if climbers went there at all nowadays. Where then were all these people going?

Rounding a corner we came to a place where the path divided. Confused, we consulted the map. John was already saying that it was the lower fork, while I argued that all the people in front of us were taking the higher one. We split up! I took the high road and arrived at a viewpoint on the top of the hill where parties of picnicking tourists and sunbathers were sprawled in the heather. I had to admit that this was not the right way to the cliff. We had never been at the top of the hill in our climbing days. We'd only gone to the cliffs in the defile.

I started to make my way down taking the shortest route, which brought me out at the top of the cliffs and there was John down below making the victory sign! I smacked my hand in acknowledgement of the mistake and ran down towards him. As I looked into the cleft I saw that it was completely deserted, clammy and cold within the narrow passage, bounded by the proverbial rock walls, where once it had been alive with people and banter. Only one lad ran through the corridor in jogging bottoms, vest and trainers.

We looked at the walls, once bare, shiny and scratched with hundreds of boots - now wet, dark and slimy, with moss growing from cracks in the rock. It felt strange to be standing there, trying to remember the past and the men who belonged there. Time had gone too quickly – and winding it back was impossible. We walked on through the defile pointing out past possible routes we vaguely remembered saying, "Was that the one we did with M---?" and "I'm sure I took the boys up that one."

A short while later, "I can't believe I climbed THAT!" followed by a wistful sigh.

"See the buttress over there," John remarked, studying the rock. "I'm sure that was the one I fell down when I was free climbing."

"You mean the time you ended up in hospital?" I said – but he didn't want to be reminded, so we moved on until we came out the other end of the gloomy passage and tramped up the hill to join the tourists. After returning to the car park we went down to Carbeth Inn nearby, where we

Liz, Torridon 1963

Anne, Torridon

Bidean's cliffs and buttresses. Glencoe.

Liz on summit of Bidean

The Cioch, Glen Brittle, Skye 1963

The Cuillins, Glen Brittle

The Dolomites, Italy. Sassolunga 1965

Alpine cattle graze beside a path, marked by number.

Liz on the way to the Contrin Hut

Contrin Hut

**Chapel behind Contrin Hut. Marmolata to rear.**

Contrin Hut annex

View of Vernardais from hut window

Jane, Susie and Liz on way to Rosengarten

The Vajolet Towers. Rosengarten.

The Grossen Stein. Langside boys and ourselves. Right (standing) - Ronnie Crawford, club leader.

The Brenta Hut

'Via Ferrata' The Bochette. Spot Liz on ladder below!

Newlands School - Parkhead, my third Glasgow school

School children enjoy a day out to Ben Bowie - Loch Lomond (early 1960's)

Children at Balmaha - Loch Lomond 1966

Above Balmaha. 'Maid of the Loch' plies Loch Lomond below.

Older boys on the Cobbler, Arrochar

Two young boys enjoying their first visit to the hills

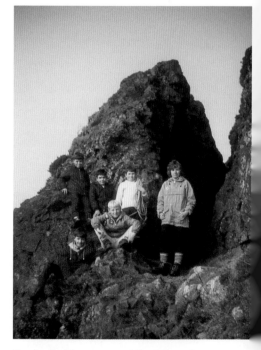

Rock climbing group at the Whangie (Liz to right)

Langside doss, Glencoe

Liz on Curved Ridge. Buachaille Etive Mor.

Hitchhiking to Glasgow from Glencoe (Liz on left)

Camping in Glencoe near Jacksonville

Old Staravclub barn, Glencoe

Starav club's new hut in Glencoe

Dolomites 1967. Cattinacio - Rosengarten.

Summit of Cattinacio. John with Davie Todd, the late John Cunningham and German tourist.

**Liz at cross on summit of Cattinacio**

**Santner Hut, Rosengarten**

**Abseiling practice, John**

**Hitchhiking. We just missed a lift!**

The Galassi Hut - Antelao

John boulder climbing near hut

Antelao. View from our highest point after the storm.

Descending ridge on Antelao. Looking north towards Cortina.

Switzerland 1969, Zermatt Station forecourt

The Bahnhof. Our accommodation in Zermatt.

The Mettelhorn. Our practice peak.

Deep pools where two glaciers meet below Monte Rosa

Monte Rosa Hut and Lyskamm

Monte Rosa Hut toilets!

An inquisitive marmot near the glacier

John on the higher slopes of Monte Rosa

Looking across the glacier to the Matterhorn from Monte Rosa. Liz.

Dawn on the Matterhorn from slopes of Monte Rosa

Schwarzsee Hotel

From Schwarzsee looking across to Monte Rosa (left) with glacier below

Sitting outside the Hornli Hut at the foot of the Matterhorn. Ron, John and Liz.

View back towards Zermatt from Hornli Hut

Tackling the Hornli Ridge. John.

The devastated forest in Chamonix 1987

La Montagne. Our accommodation.

La Montagne kitchen 1987.
Heather and Iona.

The Beau Soleil et des Guides.
Our accommodation in 1969.

Looking over Chamonix from path to Montenvers and Mer de Glace. Burning forest debris.

The Mer de Glace

Bleak October in Montenvers Station

Heather and Iona at Planpraz cable car station

sat outside at a wooden table along with dozens of bikers on a weekend run around the lowlands - changed days!

# RETURN TO GELNCOE IN 2015

As for Glencoe with its charming candlelit dosses, aroma of wood smoke and crisp bacon, and the searing, challenging peaks behind - that was another story. Once we moved to Sutherland at the beginning of the seventies I could count on one hand the number of times we'd returned there. Despite its grandeur, the area never had the same enduring magic for me as the Cairngorms with its vast plateau and its hidden secrets. Once we stopped going to Glencoe on a regular basis, it gradually faded into obscurity. We'd done most things there was to do there and a night in a doss didn't hold the appeal it once had! Driving south from Sutherland to visit relations we followed the A9, so that to go through Glencoe would require a special occasion. Nevertheless, a few years ago our daughter, Heather, moved to Oban and visiting her saw us clipping the north end of Glencoe, enough for a fleeting glimpse of the Pap near the start of the Aonach Eagach, as we crossed the bridge over Loch Leven at Ballachulish, before heading further west.

With time to spare on our way back from a recent trip we suddenly made a proposal, "Let's take a run down the glen?" I suggested. "For old times sake."

Ignoring the bridge at Ballachulish we turned right into Glencoe village and followed the back road to Clachaig. "Was that the dance hall?" I said as we passed a larger building amongst the cottages fronting the side of the road. We carried on out of the village towards the farm where the Starav Club doss had been built, but when we arrived at what we thought was the spot, it wasn't there. "Oh well," said John. "I had a feeling it might be gone. It's been years – decades in fact." We didn't get out the car. We kept going towards Clachaig. On our left the slopes were now towering above us up to the heights of the Aonach Eagach ridge.

"I don't remember those hills being so steep," I said, sucking in my breath in awe.

When we saw Clachaig Inn, some of the façade was the same, including the front door, but the rest of it had mushroomed on all sides with posh conservatories and public bar extensions. On the grass opposite which had been close cropped by sheep, there were half a dozen wooden table and bench sets where bikers were sitting with drinks.

There was one spare table so we sat down and tied the dogs to the table legs. "I'll get the drinks," said John and marched across the road, while I sat scanning the skyline on both sides of the glen. Even the path up the side of Clachaig Gully, which was where we had once accessed the ridge looked like a desperate V.S. (eg 'very severe' in rock climbing terms) and Bidean on the opposite side of the glen looked equally dramatic and invincible.

"How did we ever do these things?" I said to John when he returned with the drinks. He was equally enthralled with Clachaig Gully that rose in vertical sweeps above us and had been one of his favourite climbs. Then he lost interest and turned to his newspaper instead, while the bikers made a noisy departure down the glen accompanied by reeking exhaust fumes. There wasn't a climber to be seen. Either they were already on top of the hills or they had travelled further afield in fast cars to other less frequented climbing areas further north.

A waitress came out to clear one of the bikers' tables of its empty glasses, but she never came back for the rest. Ten minutes later I was bored looking into the back of John's newspaper so I went across to the vacated tables and cleared all the empty glasses myself, then I staggered across the road to the bar with them, trying not to trip as I crossed from the grass to the tarmac down a rough slope. When I entered the bar the attendant looked up and said in an American accent, "Wow! Thank you so much for that. You can have a job anytime."

I blushed, saying, "I wish." Couldn't she see that I was more than seventy years old?

I tried to bite my tongue before the next sentence came out, but it came anyway – "I used to climb here many years ago, about fifty to be exact, and we came to the public bar at Clachaig for a drink on Saturday nights before going to the dance."

"Oh really," she said with a beaming smile. "Feel free to look around. The public bar is just around the corner through that door," she waved her hand behind her.

This was exactly what I wanted. I lost no time in dashing through the door. The little room I remembered had expanded considerably in size, with new matching rustic wooden furniture, boxed cutlery, napkins and condiment sets, and there were cheap pub advertisements on the walls, although it was pleasing to also see a few references to mountaineering and the Inn's historic past.

I walked slowly back outside and found John still immersed in the daily newspaper. "Come on," I said. "It's time we were going – back to Sutherland, where we belong."

# 4

## HITCHHIKING EPICS

## TYNDRUM

Hitchhiking was a way of life in the sixties for many climbers, walkers and weekenders who didn't have cars, particularly for the Glasgow mob who regularly headed to the North West on a Friday night. We nearly always made it from Balloch to our destination in Glencoe or Arrochar, even Fort William on occasions, but there were times when it just wasn't possible. To be stranded late at night, in the dark and bad weather, without a vehicle in sight was soul destroying and demanded action to do something about our predicament, which meant looking for an emergency doss. This happened twice during my hitching days and the first time was at Tyndrum.

I had set off with Jim on a cold, wet and dreich winter's night. Not even the worst of winter weather would prevent us from trying to reach Glencoe, but on this occasion we were stumped at Tyndrum. It was approaching midnight and the rain had turned to sleet, accompanied by a driving wind. There was no traffic and we had no tent so the only answer was a doss. Tyndrum Hotel was nearby but it was closed. There was a rough pull in area next to it and tucked in at the side was what looked like a gypsy cart or a road wagon of some description. Jim marched over to it and wrenched open a side door, then he beckoned me over saying, "This will do for the night."

I peered into the inky gloom over his shoulder, and shone my torch around the interior. "You must be joking," I said in disgust. "It's filthy – and there's heaps of coal on the floor!"

"I'll soon shift that," he replied. "It's better than nothing – don't you think?"

I raised my eyebrows, while he hefted himself inside, grabbed a bundle of scrunched up, discarded newspapers and swept the coal to one side, creating more dust in the process. I stood outside fuming and fervently hoping that a late night vehicle would still appear and rescue us from this unsavoury predicament. There were various classes of dosses and this one was definitely at the lower end of the scale, discounting caves and underneath bridges.

I had to admit though that it was better than continuing to walk in the dark, the wind and the drenching sleet, with only Bridge of Orchy and the wild emptiness of the Rannoch Moor ahead. We scrambled inside, shut the door and unrolled our sleeping bags on the cleanest part of the floor.

In the morning we wakened early and as we were near the hotel where a side door was now open, I hurried across with my sponge bag to get a wash. When I re-emerged five minutes later and looked across to the road wagon I was taken aback to see smoke coming out the chimney. Dashing over, I burst inside shouting, "What are you doing? Someone's going to see this smoke and investigate."

"I was only burning the old newspapers and some other rubbish in the stove," he said, raising his eyebrows at my outburst.

"And don't you think someone else is going to see it and complain?" I insisted.

Well someone else did, because the door suddenly burst open behind me and I whipped round to see a burly red faced road worker in the frame. "What's going on?" he exploded.

I was suddenly stuck for words. Talk about being caught red handed, but the absurdity of the situation got the better of me and all I could do was laugh uncontrollably.

Jim tried to apologise and explain our predicament, but at this point the road worker also seemed to relent. He smirked broadly and walked away muttering, "Bloomin' hikers", while at the same time I thought I saw a ghost of a smile.

# BRIDGE OF ORCHY

My next emergency bothy escapade occurred with John after we were engaged and took place at Bridge of Orchy, about six miles north of Tyndrum. We were similarly benighted on a cold, dark, wet evening with no signs of a lift appearing, when John suggested dossing in a hut on the nearby railway line. We tramped up to have a look and found the hut beside the track. The door was tied with string, but we undid the knot and stepped inside, shining our torches around the room. In comparison to the road workers' wagon at Tyndrum it was decidedly more presentable, but there was a large gas cylinder in one corner that had a whiff of gas around it. "Well if you can put that cylinder outside the door, it'll do fine," I said, wrinkling my nose at the smell.

He duly hefted it outside and we spread out our belongings on the wooden floor. It wasn't as late as the Tyndrum episode, being just after 9 o'clock, but we were tired hanging around and had decided to call it a day, also Bridge of Orchy Hotel was nearby and open until 10 o'clock so we thought a drink in the public bar would go down well.

It was great craic there as all the local worthies seemed to be out for a weekend bevy, and the stories they were recounting were hilarious. Amongst their number was an older guy, a retired railway employee, who brought up the subject of the railway bothys positioned at intervals along the track. "The bothys used to be locked," he said, "and people were always breaking into them, but the funny thing is, now that they're left open, nobody bothers."

John and I looked at each other and I could feel my face glowing scarlet with guilt, but we said nothing. Then in case anyone should have noticed our sudden silence we asked if the winter skiing had started in Glencoe.

When we left half an hour later we sniggered all the way up the hill to the track. On our arrival at the hut we stepped inside, tied the door shut from the inside and made ready for the night. Initially we slept, but some time later I must have wakened, and lying there in my sleeping bag in the inky blackness I was suddenly aware of a strange, muffled noise. Gradually it became louder and more pronounced, being composed of a slow whining 'squeak – pink – clink' that repeated itself with monotonous regularly. "What's that noise?" I said to John, poking him awake as I sat upright and listened with baited breath. The laboured squeaks and clinking were increasing in volume. Something nasty was coming out of the darkness to get us?

John was also listening as the escalating, pronounced squeaks suddenly stopped right outside our accommodation. I held my breath as the sudden silence was followed by several thumps and scrunching in the gravel as footsteps approached the door of the hut. John grabbed his trousers as muffled voices sounded right outside the door and someone fiddled with the handle. This was followed by a shout. "Who left that gas cylinder outside?"

Then another angry voice announced, "Someone's tied the door from the inside!"

I froze as John stood up fumbling for the catch on his breeches, then there was a massive shove from outside. The door burst open and several hefty overnight track maintenance employees arrived in the middle of our boudoir!

I'm not sure who was the most aghast, but both parties were momentarily speechless.

Horrors! We'd been caught red handed! The track employees recovered first, while we gasped in shock, blinking in the glare of their head torches. I was still clutching my sleeping bag, but John was standing and I could see that his breeches were on inside out, with the tell tale pocket linings flapping like a pair of wings.

"And where have you two come from?" muttered the first man to regain his breath.

We started to explain ourselves in an embarrassed rush, but when they realised we were stranded hikers from Glasgow, not vandals or looters, they relented and left us to it, with a gruff request to replace the gas cylinder where we'd found it after we departed.

After they'd gone, squeaking and pinking on down the line in their works line trolley, I looked at John and we dissolved in stitches. "Well that was a near one," I said. "We really must save up and get ourselves an old banger."

Not long after that episode we became the proud owners of our own grey mini van, which gave us scope to visit many new areas. Things were changing. We were becoming members of the more affluent society, with duvet jackets, Jo Brown packs and Icelandic sleeping bags – but first of all we had a big summer expedition planned to the Dolomites in Italy. I had been raring to go back there again and I wanted to show them to John who was now my fiancé.

# PART 4: RETURN TO THE DOLOMITES 1967

# 1

# THE ROSENGARTEN

It was two years before I had an opportunity to return to the Dolomites. Now being engaged to John we spent more time as a couple on the hills and less attached to a group, making our own decisions on where to spend weekends and holidays. John had so far not been to the continent and as I was never done extolling the virtues of the Dolomites to him it was decided we should make it our summer holiday in 1967. We planned two weeks in July, with the first week being spent in the Rosengarten, which was one of the most thrilling regions I had previously visited, while for the second week we selected a new area in the vicinity of Cortina, which at one time had been a winter Olympics venue.

In 1965 all travel arrangements from London had been made by the Langside, but this time we would have to do it ourselves. Aiming to do things on the cheap we hitchhiked to London and stayed for a couple of nights with Jean, my old school friend, with whom I had once walked the Lairig Ghru in 1962. While in the capital we sought to fix up travel insurance for mountaineering abroad which was not easy, but we daren't go without it. Any mention of mountaineering activities in holiday insurance company offices met with a quick refusal, but at the last minute we achieved success with the Austrian Alpine Club at their London headquarters. It entailed having to become members of the club first which made us feel important and even our impressive membership cards decorated with eidelweiss gave us the added satisfaction that we were on a mission, although we knew we had to be extra careful so as not to have to call upon their financial services!

After travelling by Cross Channel Ferry and two trans-continental trains, one of them being overnight, we arrived in Bolzano in Northern Italy just in time to catch a late afternoon bus to Pozza di Fassa where there was a campsite. We had more luggage than on my previous visit as we'd included a tent and other necessary camping gear, thinking it would save money on hut fees, but it was a false economy as the increased weight, coupled with the Italian heat made back packing extremely tiresome and led to disgruntled exchanges! Well who knows, we might be disengaged by the end of the holiday! The extra freedom that camping gave us had to be measured against extra work, a harder bed and perhaps less social life in comparison to what one might encounter in a hut, although huts could also present disadvantages, as we found out later in Cortina.

After striking camp in Pozza we got the cable car to Caimpedie and walked from there, through the forest into the Rosengarten for our first week. It was great to be back after two years, seeing the impressive bulk of Cattinacio again which the highest mountain in the area, and the stunning Vajolet Towers appearing in the distance. We also passed the Grossen Stein where the Langside boys had stayed and as there was a convenient grassy meadow opposite we decided to set up camp there.

It was late afternoon by the time we'd finished organising our campsite and despite our stack of food supplies we decided to take a walk up the cliff path to visit the hut I'd previously stayed in and have a plate of good Italian minestrone, in addition to socializing and finding out who was in the area. On the way we looked into the cave under the Grossen Stein, but there was no sign of life there, despite packs and belongings stashed at the back. We hoped they might belong to Scots and shortly after arriving at the hut we discovered this was the case! Not only that, the three men involved were from Glasgow and well known to us from weekending in Glencoe, being John Cunningham and Davie Todd from the Creag Dhu Mountaineering Club along with associate member, Dave Brown who had once come up through the Langside. We were pleased to meet up with these guys because they were good company in the evening and owing to their superior knowledge of the Dolomites they were able to suggest routes that we might manage to accomplish on the rock for our level of experience, without boasting about their own ambitious and superior plans!

Our first acclimatization project was the via ferrata that I had done with Jane in 1965 round the back of Cattinacio, which gave us a chance to get a birds eye view of the whole area, including close-up views of the towers that we were hoping to tackle. This was to be no ordinary walking holiday as opposed to my previous trip with the Langside girls. It was to be decidedly more ambitious, but as I drank in the sight of these high exposed and extremely perpendicular towers again, I had a twinge of anxiety at what we were planning to do. I was now twenty-six years old and not quite as reckless or fearless as I once was, not to mention the fact that the via ferrata I had romped up two years ago had completely exhausted me. This I put down to insufficient training beforehand and the long journey from Scotland without sufficient acclimatization. As we sipped refreshments outside the high Santner Hut we had an excellent view of the three iconic towers that gave their name to the area. They were reported to be easier than they looked, due to the rough limestone rock with plenty of holds, but the information had not exactly boosted my confidence, despite the Glasgow boys recommending that we try tower number three, called Torre Winkler, the lowest of the group. They had also advised that we try the route via normale to the summit of Cattinacio, said to have a few relatively straight forward rock pitches mixed with scrambling, although a rope would be advisable on account of the exposure involved.

Despite my obsession with mountains I was not aiming to be a VS (Very Severe standard) rock climber, and I was beginning to wonder if I'd brought some anxiety on myself by suggesting we have a proper mountaineering holiday in the Dolomites. The other crucial matter concerning the towers was that supposing we reached the top, the only way down was to abseil, which would involve several long rope lengths and far too much space below our feet.

In the morning the weather was perfect as we gathered our gear for an attempt on Torre Winkler - rope, slings and pitons - and set off on the steep rock strewn path that led from the Vajolet Hut to the base of the towers. The Winkler was the first of these and drawing level with it we scrambled across to the base and roped up with a flutter of excitement. This was the real McCoy now. I was committed, but at least John was leading.

Initially the rough texture of the rock and the superfluity of holds gave a false sense of security. This would be OK I decided, as long as I didn't look down, and the next tower was comfortingly close, so that looking across the gap towards it was reassuring. After all looking at solid rock was better than looking into outer space. We progressed upwards for several pitches, belaying from ledges with strong belay points, but we were so engrossed in the climb that we failed to notice something unpleasant was brewing high above us – something not on the rock at all – but up in the sky behind us. A thunderstorm was gathering ammunition for battle – and Dolomite thunderstorms could be horrendously explosive. It was definitely not something one would want to be caught out in, especially on the exposure of a high Dolomite tower!

We heard the low ominous rumble first and looking up we noticed how menacingly dark the sky had become, not too far from our present position. The sun had disappeared – then we saw a brilliant flash in the middle distance. It wouldn't be long before it arrived overhead. I cringed at the sudden enormity of our situation, and shouted up to John.

With unspoken agreement we started to rope down, abseiling between belay points as hastily as possible. The thought of being an exposed target on the tower in a fast approaching electric storm was a frightening proposition. It would be bad enough to be caught out in the valley in such a storm, let alone on the tower. We redoubled our descending efforts as rolls of thunder became louder and more menacing, with less time between each, although the usual accompanying torrential rain was still holding off.

It was with a huge sense of relief that we finally jumped down onto the rough ground at the base of the tower, just as the first splats of rain started, and joined a group of other scurrying climbers trailing coils of rope, all of whom had abandoned climbs on the towers. We crossed the intervening scree fields at a gallop, making for the shelter of the nearest available hut, which was the Alberto, situated midway between the Vajolet Hut and the Santner. It was not one I had previously visited.

By the time we reached the front door rain was lashing and the thunder almost above us, as we fell into the front porch amongst a pack of other people and soaking wet clothes. We'd been carrying the rope bundled between us and we threw it onto the floor as we collapsed onto the nearest bench, trying to regain our breath. Other climbers and high level walkers were still squashing in behind us as the thunder finally arrived directly overhead – and the drama that followed was unbelievable.

Rain poured down the outside of the steamy windows and water was rushing and splashing down the steep sided valley beyond, while above us I thought the roof was coming down. It was the most ear splitting and explosive storm I'd ever heard. Each thunderous crash overhead was like a bomb going off, followed by machine fire rebounding and echoing off the surrounding rock walls, accompanied by showers of noisy flying missiles smashing against the rocks below. I was loathe to look outside in case something enormous had fallen down and was about to engulf us. It was like a war zone with brilliant yellow and purple lightning flashes slicing through the sky, illuminating the scene for a few seconds at a time, bouncing off numerous projections in the valley before the scene plunged into gloom again. I was half expecting the hut to be targeted and the roofing materials to land at my feet – or a strong blast of hurricane force wind to sweep inside, signifying that we had been holed and were about to be swept away to imminent disaster?

Despite the futility of such a decision I nose dived onto the floor under a nearby table, in succession to a particularly volatile explosion, self preservation having taken precedence against reason – then I felt embarrassed because none of the men were doing that! They were still upstanding, animatedly watching the drama through the windows, shouting and pointing at things outside and seemingly oblivious to the racket. It wasn't as if I hadn't seen a Dolomite thunderstorm before two years ago, but the difference was I'd never seen one in such a barren rock area, without trees or vegetation to cushion the effects, never mind the noise.

In twenty minutes it stopped, almost as suddenly as it had started. Blue sky returned above us and those packed inside the hut started to stream back outside, laughing and joking at the intensity of it all, and preparing to scramble back across the valley to the towers to resume interrupted climbs.

We also went outside and surveyed the scene. There were no signs of fresh rock devastations in the valley or fallen masonry around the hut, and the towers were still standing as boldly as ever, like they had done for hundreds of years. As we watched the other parties hurrying across to the towers I said to John. "Well I don't know about you, but I fancy a plate of minestrone down at the Vajolet Hut."

I'd had enough excitement for one day and John willingly complied with the suggestion. Despite the briefness of the drama that had unfolded, I felt slightly shaken by our close encounter with the forces of nature and as I continually squinted back at the terrifying height of the towers above, I was just a little bit relieved that the storm had given us an excuse to abandon the project! I was never one hundred percent sure exactly what John's feelings were on the subject, but the soup with its extra appetising helping of parmesan cheese swirling in the centre was decidedly refreshing and much appreciated, as we planned our next projects for the rest of our time in the Rosengarten.

Next day we decided to replenish our provisions which involved a trip down to Vigo di Fassa, the nearest village, walking to Caimpedie and using the cable car from there. During the walk we passed a spectacular sight. A party of young people, about one hundred strong were marching one behind the other on the path through the meadows towards the towers ahead, with a local priest in the lead and all singing in unison as they tramped along. The song had an Alpine flair with snatches of yodelling and reminded me of the musical 'The Sound of Music', when the Von Trapp children crossed the mountains from Austria into Switzerland. It was like a weekend pilgrimage and had an entrancing, hypnotic feel to it, making us want to join in, like we were following the pied piper of Hamelin, despite the fact that we were heading in the opposite direction. It also reminded me of the time in Glasgow when on route back to the school from an Easter service in church, the children sang 'Dance, dance, wherever you may be, I am the Lord of the dance said he,' for the entire journey.

When we reached Vigo we were unexpectedly treated to another spectacle of a completely different nature. We were walking in the main street when we noticed a couple pushing a rustic wooden cart up the hill with a large bundle resting inside, when suddenly the barrow coggled over a rough patch in the road and upended itself. The bundle on board bounced out of the cart and rolled away at speed, while the middle aged couple in charge promptly started a very vocal slanging match for all to hear, accompanied by finger pointing, fist waving and cries of 'Stupido! Stupido!' It was like something in a film set but we felt obliged to carry on walking on the other side of the road, trying not to draw attention to the fact that we found the incident hilarious.

It came on rain as we returned on the trek through the forest into the open meadows around Caimpedie, lugging the shopping in our rucksacks. Nor was it a short, sharp shower, but a persistent heavy drizzle which soaked us before we regained our tent, not to mention our washing I'd left out on a makeshift line in the morning. The evening didn't promise much of an improvement so we decided rather than sit in a wet tent, to walk up to the hut.

On route we called at the Grossen Stein, but only Dave was in residence. When we told him of our intentions he decided to join us and we were soon sitting with large platefuls of spaghetti, sprinkled with parmesan cheese and tomato sauce. So much for our shopping expedition!

John and I made plans for the following day which were for the ascent of Cattinacio, weather permitting. Considering our view of the mountain from the tent it seemed like an over ambitious project, but the Grossen Stein tigers of the sport had assured us the much easier rock route up the back was entirely do-able for our level of experience, although there was a moderate amount of exposure.

However, our ascent was postponed for another day due to extremely low cloud and more persistent soft rain which was a different matter entirely from the short, sharp thunderstorms. The hut was full of disenchanted, grounded climbers in the morning, but the Italians always made the best of things, usually by lusty singing, climbing discussions and stories, eating and drinking and cards. It fared up in the afternoon, but by that time it was too late to tackle major routes. Bouldering problems in the vicinity of the hut then came into force, while John and I rigged up an abseil into a rocky gorge to practice technique. It was slightly upstream from the hut and our campsite and we were horrified to see a rubbish dump spilling into the stream, comprising rusting tin cans, old shoes and other assorted items of surplus kitchen equipment - and this self same water was passing our tent. We had been using it for drinking and cooking with the addition of one sterilization tablet, but we decided to add several in future!

We only had two days remaining in the Rosengarten and fortunately the next one was dry and bright, so we gathered our gear immediately after breakfast and set off for the Santner Hut, heading for the Route via Normale on Cattinacio. As we surveyed it from below we were pleased to see good holds but we roped up for safety. There was plenty of exposure as we climbed, but the most annoying thing was passing people descending on the same route and trying not to get the ropes tangled. Once on the summit ridge there was a lofty, somewhat scary and exposed scramble to achieve the summit and you were very aware of height when you looked around and noticed the miniscule huts in the depths far below.

The summit was marked by the usual cross and at the bottom of it there was a small cupboard where the log book was kept to record ascents - and who should be sitting relaxing behind the cross but John Cunningham and Davie Todd, having just completed a seriously difficult climb up the face. We were thrilled to meet up with them in such an elevated vantage point and we photographed each other at the cross for posterity. Sadly John C was later killed in a mountaineering accident involving a sea rescue off the coast of Britain so I treasure that photograph of the great occasion when we all met on the summit of Rosengarten's highest peak.

Back at the Vajolet Hut in the late afternoon, I still seemed to be possessed of boundless energy, so while John went off to do boulder problems with the boys I said I would explore on my own. I still craved the odd solo expedition, a throw back to the days of my youth in Perthshire, and I wanted to venture up another valley beyond our hut that I had not so far explored, leading to a high pass with unknown territory on the other side. My goals in the past had always been to see what lay over the horizon and this was what I intended to do, never mind the fact it generally turned out to be more of the same!

On my map there was a hut marked at the top of the pass called Principe, but it was further away than I thought. Despite the time escalating I doggedly kept going until I reached my objective. The hut was unique, being constructed on a shelf, squashed under a cliff of overhanging rock, while a line of washing was fluttering in the breeze close beside it. There was music coming from the hut which prompted me to investigate inside and as soon as I opened the door I was welcomed in with several offers of a drink, while lusty singing to the sound of mouth organs and table thumpings continued all around me. I wanted to stay for the evening, but it had begun to rain and was growing dusk, making me realise I'd better return to the Vajolet Hut before I was reported missing.

When I arrived at half past nine in semi-darkness John was somewhat miffed, but he was sitting with the Creag Dhu boys who were making enquiries from another guy about a climb on the Torre Piaz, which they were contemplating later in the week. They were interrupted by the hut keeper who appeared at this point insisting that everybody try the National drink of Grappa, as he had just opened a bottle. It was like the equivalent of Scots Whisky, but decidedly stronger, and it was considered rude to refuse it. I didn't like whisky so I certainly wasn't trying the Grappa and fortunately I got away with my polite refusal, but the rest of the company accepted, some grimacing with unexpected shock as the fiery liquid touched their throat!

The hut keeper looked upon the semi regular Glasgow climbers as good custom and when it later came on a persistent deluge he offered accommodation in a spare room in the attic, which would save us getting soaked returning to the tent and the Grossen Stein in darkness. We took him up on his offer immediately, relishing the chance of a night in a comfortable bunk, but overnight I dreamed that the Creag Dhu had got up and abseiled out the bedroom window in their underwear, which caused a laugh when I described it later at the breakfast table!

As far as John and I were concerned it was our last day in the area and most of it was spent preparing for our move to Cortina.

# 2

# CORTINA AND ANTELAO

To save money we decided to hitchhike down to Cortina, but our second lift from an Italian who seemed to be in treating the roads as a racing circuit, crazily speeding round hairpin bends only inches from precipitous drops, rather put us off! Our last lift was from a public service bus!

Once in Cortina which was a fairly large town, we looked out for the local campsite, and having spotted a sign for this in several languages, we followed an arrow which led to the outskirts of a residential area to the south. When we finally arrived at the designated place we found the site to be palatial, boasting a fantastic open air swimming pool, a well stocked shop and luxurious restaurant, set in landscaped woodland. It appeared to be a touring site for up market caravans and superior stylish tents with multiple rooms, not a climbers' camp, but we could raise our game when necessary! We booked it for the week.

On our first full day we had a blast with two sessions in the outdoor pool, a three-course meal in the restaurant and a stroll down to the Winter Olympic Park to see the ski jump. Whoever would have thought we were on a mountaineering holiday? We were tourists for the day - but the ultimate aim was to fit in a climb of some notable eminence in the area. The peaks were not quite so perpendicular, or in such close proximity to our accommodation as previously, and to reach them would involve public transport or thumbing a lift. Nevertheless we had already earmarked one to the south, which was visible from a bridge near our campsite. It was possibly ten miles distant, pyramid shaped, with snow on the summit and had an aura of something special about it.

We checked it out on our map and identified it as Antelao, which was 3263 metres in height - 10,701 feet, and with the nearest township being St Vito di Cadore. We trained binoculars onto the peak, noticing extensive forestry on the lower slopes, leading up to rock and snow. It was the shape that attracted us, similar to the Matterhorn in Switzerland. We decided to make enquiries about Antelao in one of the numerous outdoor shops in Cortina.

The mountaineering specialists in the town were Aladdin's caves, displaying the best Alpine equipment available, making us wish we had a fat purse, instead of a tight budget. We found an assistant who could speak English and asked him about Antelao. 'Yes, it will be possible', he replied. 'but you need crampons.' We were not sure whether this was absolutely necessary or whether he was trying for a sale, but I did feel it was time I got crampons of my own, instead of borrowing as previously. Mountaineering gear in Italy was cheaper than in Britain at that time and of very good quality, as well as being much in demand due to the extent of the Alps in Europe and the growing popularity of the sport. We hesitated. After deliberation I selected a pair of 12 point Grivels which included front points, engineered by the Italian, Laurent Grivel, to speed up ice climbing, along with reduction of laborious step cutting. Meanwhile John purchased a new ice axe to replace his North Wall Hammer, invaluable for stability and arresting a fall.

Feeling considerably lighter of purse after these extravagances, we hurried out the door to avoid further temptation and spent the evening in the campsite pool. It was becoming difficult to tell whether climbing or swimming was the more addictive on this holiday.

The following day was spent with a mixture of swimming, walking and planning for our two day expedition to Antelao, which entailed leaving our tent and some belongings at the site, but our Dutch neighbours said they would keep an eye on things for us. We didn't have a climbers' guide book for the region, but our map showed the paths which threaded the forests towards our objective from St Vito and it also marked a convenient mountain hut called the Galassi Rifugio, right at the base of Antelao. We were in good spirits and didn't anticipate any difficulties.

In order to have two full days we left the campsite early in the morning and hitchhiked to St Vito with no problem. Locating of the tracks through the forest was next on the agenda, and according to the map there were two, one on either side of the Secco River, and they appeared to join forces higher in the valley. We decided that the one to the left was more used and possibly shorter so we set off, hoping to reach the hut, which at a rough calculation was six kilometres distant, before the full glare of the midday sun. The approach also involved considerable climbing and we had packs to carry with all essential gear and a change of clothes.

However, our chosen track started to deteriorate as we climbed, turning into an evasive, meandering footpath, with encroaching vegetation, some of which was hanging across the path. By this time we had gained some height and were reluctant to turn back, which would waste valuable time, with no certainty that the other path would be any better. We were consoled by the fact that the two paths were supposed to join up so we doggedly kept going until we came to a clearance in the forest where our dwindling path disappeared into a field of waist high grass.

John at this stage pointed out that if the worst came about we could strike back through the forest in a beeline for the Secco River and after crossing it by some means or other, negotiate the forest on the other side to pick up the second path. Having seen the density of the forest in that direction I wasn't much in favour of the proposal, so we carried on tramping through the field with now no sign of any path at all. The situation was ripe for a heated argument, but before this could develop I said, "Well - we're explorers – are we not? Let's go for your suggestion and break through the jungle ahead towards the Secco River."

We sweated in the heat of the rising sun, despite plunging back into the forest, and started to fight our way through the trees towards the river. We could hear it and knew it was close, but the ground beneath our feet was now presenting a problem. The gradient had escalated, besides being unstable, while there were unexpected holes and a succession of sharp prickly branches sprang back at exposed flesh. "This is ridiculous!"

I said to John with an edge to my voice.

Sometimes we had to pull ourselves up a steep incline, hanging onto the overhead branches for assistance and at other times we used them to swing across deep muddy ditches. We became completely lost and disorientated, sometimes thinking we'd found a suggestion of a path, then discovering we hadn't. At this point we were both looking for something upon which to vent our wrath. "You said take the left fork," John accused.

"No I didn't," came the hot reply. "We both decided that was the one!"

"It's the map that's wrong," he continued, bringing in a third party and looking like he was ready to tear it up.

In the face of no other ideas as to how to extricate ourselves from our predicament we carried on, fuming, with conversation at a standstill, before catching a welcome sight of the river below us. It appeared to be in a ravine because we now had to slither down a muddy, almost perpendicular embankment to reach it. As there was no alternative we grasped the overhead branches again and started swinging from one to another like monkeys, while at the same time trying to keep our footing in the slippery mud below, and attempting to prevent our packs from getting snagged in overhead foliage. During this performance our clothes became covered in needles, while some went down our neck, got tangled up in our hair and hung in clumps from our socks! We thought we saw another suggestion of a path at one point, but it pulled up short and disappeared down a waterfall.

Most of the morning was now gone. Whose idea had it been to climb Antelao anyway? After much concentrated effort and cursing under our breath we reached the water's edge lower down, where the river was fortunately neither too wide or too deep to ford. We managed to get across without too much hassle, but once on the other side we had to scramble up a high embankment, hanging onto tree roots to keep from sliding back. After this strenuous performance we found ourselves in more dense forest, but suddenly a ray of light appeared and shortly afterwards we burst unexpectedly out of the jungle and were astonished to find ourselves facing a wide double track, this being the right hand fork that without local knowledge we had neglected to try!

To say we were exasperated with our mistake was a complete understatement, for we had wasted two hours struggling through the forest on the opposite side of the river and had not gained much height above St Vito to match such Herculean efforts! To add insult to injury the sun was now roasting and we still had a long trek to reach the hut. In fact it took us a total of five hours to complete the approach walk, which was reputed to be two hours under normal circumstances - following the correct path!

When we finally saw the Galassi Hut appearing at the head of the pass, it was nothing like we had imagined, and nothing like the previous Alpine Huts we had experienced with their wide balconies and often expansive shady overhanging timber roofs. It was more like a prison reminiscent of World War Two, being a long three storey building of depressing grey stone, with rows of tiny matching windows and dark green shutters. Due to the small windows and the absence of electric light within, the interior was dark and gloomy and it took a few minutes for our eyes to become accustomed enough to the darkness to find the hut warden's office.

The said gentleman had very limited English, but he understood our request for accommodation in the cheapest category and led us to a room with straw mattresses on the floor.

We discovered that postcards of Antelao were sold in the reception hall, with the normal route of ascent marked in white, so we bought one and studied it. The white line ascended a steep and stony valley to the right of the hut, before proceeding up an almost vertical cliff face in a series of tight zig zags, to access a long steep ridge, which was partly covered in snow in its higher sections. The final cone some considerable distance above was marked and described as being 3,263 metres in height, but it was not quite clear if the concluding stages of ascent might

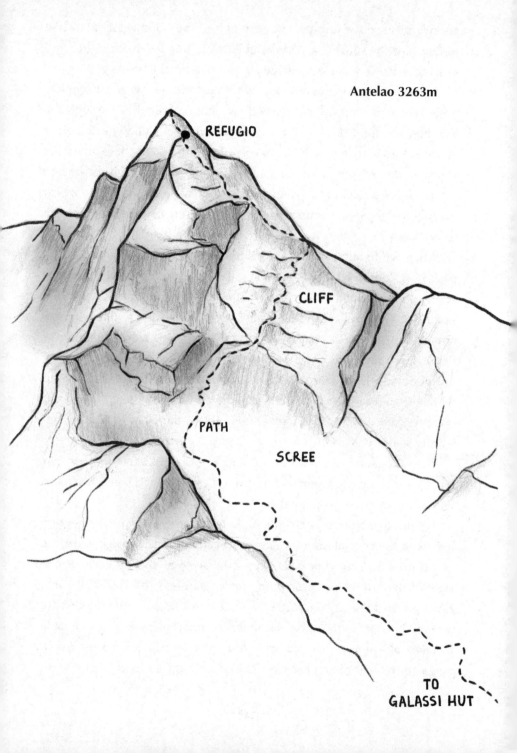

Antelao 3263m

REFUGIO

CLIFF

PATH

SCREE

TO
GALASSI HUT

be hiding some last minute obstacles.

We were glad of our rope, ice axes and crampons and spent the remainder of the afternoon outside, squinting up at the lofty summit, trying to convince ourselves that it was doable, before exploring the terrain in close proximity to the hut, including tackling a few boulder problems nearby.

When the sun started to die down we went indoors to investigate the hut menu. It didn't appear to be a very well used establishment in comparison to others we had frequented and the menu was limited and somewhat indecipherable. We eventually ordered 'wurstal con crauti' after having looked it up in our phrase book and found it to contain sausage with cabbage, which was the least innocuous dish on the menu. When it arrived the sausage was enormous and slightly suspicious looking, while the pile of accompanying soggy cabbage was liberally drenched in vinegar, which neither John nor I liked! Later on we ordered a roll with salami, but the roll was tough and the salami like leather!

The day had started badly with our debacle in the forest, but unknown to us at the time, our venture was about to get a whole lot worse, for completely different and unexpected reasons.

A few other visitors, mostly men, lurked in dark corners of the hut, conversing in languages we couldn't understand. Amongst these was a seedy-looking Italian, slightly older than ourselves, who was talking to the hut keeper in slurred tones, while intermittently slugging from a bottle of spirits, possibly Grappa. Occasionally they glanced in our direction and pointed, which made us feel uneasy. We decided to repair to our accommodation, but on the way we had to pass these men and the shifty Italian customer intercepted us. He seemed to be making a request, the nature of which was incomprehensible, despite frantic hand waving which he was using as an aid to enlighten us.

At this point the hut keeper's teenage son who could speak German stepped forward to provide assistance. I rustled up my limited tourist German as an aid to communication, but it was insufficient to get to the bottom of the matter and merely added to the confusion. Then suddenly another gentleman approached us from the shadows - older and smartly dressed. "Can I help you?" he said in accented English. "I speak English and Italian."

We immediately fell upon him with relief and asked him to find out what the booze swigging Italian wanted from us. He nodded and obliged, before turning back towards us saying, "I believe you are to be climbing Antelao tomorrow? He wants to go with you and share your rope."

"What?" we gasped, utterly dumb founded at this revelation. The plan had been to go on our own, and although we might have welcomed some knowledgeable company to guide us, this individual did not fit into that category. As well as being slightly intoxicated and eccentric, he didn't have his own equipment, and had no more knowledge of the route than we had, never mind the fact that his abilities for such an ascent were completely unknown to us. He would be a liability. We would be responsible for his safety as well as our own, and if he suddenly insisted on going back or taking a different direction we were scuppered.

As firmly as we could we said, "No! No!" frantically trying to think of an excuse to back up our refusal, but it was useless. He was determined. Then he turned on his heel and disappeared towards the staircase for the dormitories, weaving an unsteady path as he went and taking another slurp from his bottle on the way. Our translator shook his head and warned us that he was intending to meet us in the morning for the ascent, at the first light of dawn.

We were speechless. Would it be possible to slip out before the dawn? How had we got into this mess? Then we felt mean. Was he just a lonely guy looking for a companion? The trouble was – climbing in the Alps was a dangerous game. We couldn't afford to risk an accident – and taking him with us was not an act of compassion, it was an act of extreme foolhardiness. We began to wish we'd never caught sight of Antelao in the first place, for it had been nothing but trouble from the start. We retired to the dormitory upset and angry, and slept little, dreading the morning.

At half past four we rose and looked out the window. It was raining! Good. The expedition had been doomed the minute we'd set out from St Vito so maybe this was our chance to call it off. Nevertheless, the skies were clear again after a few minutes so we felt we had no further reasons to procrastinate, collected our equipment and clomped downstairs. Unfortunately the Italian was waiting for us and seemed to be sober. We signed to him to wait while we had coffee and nodded towards the window where the skies had clouded over again and more rain was looming on the horizon. However, it didn't materialize and we knew we had no more excuses not to set off.

Reluctantly we signed towards the Italian and with a heavy heart we trudged up the barren valley, with our companion keeping up surprisingly well in the rear. The final decision would be taken when we reached the cliff that led to the ridge, because after that we were more or less committed. The cliff had looked intimidating from afar, but on closer inspection it appeared reasonable, almost like a via ferrata and there were plenty of holds.

Our unwanted companion resolutely kept pace and we reached the ridge above which was fairly broad, barren and stony, with snow here and there in sheltered hollows. It reared upwards in a continual sweep towards the summit, which was partly obscured in cloud some considerable distance away. There were dips and gullies between, possibly hiding unexpected obstacles.

Much to our dismay the clouds were accumulating and rolling down the ridge towards us. Then suddenly it was snowing, with heavy flurries approaching in our direction, propelled by a strengthening wind. I'd just known this whole trip was going to be a catastrophe. The Italian was standing with his back to us and much to my chagrin I saw him furtively replacing a metallic flask into an inside pocket in his jacket.

"This is all we need," I said to John in dismay. We kept walking, but soon we were in thick cloud. What if we lost him in the mist? We'd be responsible. It didn't bear thinking about. Maybe we should be roped? We were high up on the mountain in bad weather and it was time to make a sensible decision. If we'd even been able to communicate with our strange companion it would have helped!

During our browsing amongst the hut literature and various maps the previous night we had discovered that Antelao boasted a small refuge on its upper slopes, at a height of about 3150 metres (10,332 feet), which could be used as a basic shelter in weather such as we were presently experiencing. We calculated it was not too far from our present position, on the left, and steering the Italian in that direction we were eventually fortunate enough to spot it.

Its position was precarious, balanced on a narrow shelf of rock above a vertical drop and secured to the cliff wall above by stout wire hawsers. Our companion forged ahead at this point, on a narrow access path bounded by a rail, which led to the door. After releasing the catch we found ourselves in a narrow room reminiscent of a railway compartment, with a bunk on either side and a few basic emergency provisions on a shelf above. The window on the left hand side looked out into a whiteout of wind driven snow and was partly covered in frost. The Italian immediately fell onto the right hand bunk and we saw him fumbling inside his jacket for the flask which he clasped to his lips, slurping greedily. We were aghast. What if he became incapable of continuing with the expedition, or of getting back down again, which seemed the more likely outcome of our adventure at the moment?

Unaware of the consternation he was causing he held the flask out to us, which we promptly refused. Without being able to talk or reason with him in his own language we felt we'd been backed into a corner. Were we now going to be trapped in this dismal tin shack on the edge of the mountain, which was only a few hundred feet from the summit? Everything now depended on the weather and the state of our bizarre companion. Should we grab his flask and hurl it down the mountain to make sure he was still in control of his legs for walking? Perhaps not –

that might precipitate angry confrontation?

We sweated uncomfortably at the thought of the predicament we had walked into and prayed hard for the storm outside to cease. Every so often I yanked open the cabin door for a better look, while John kept the window free of condensation and the Italian furtively cradled his flask like his life depended on it. Waves of apprehension continued to shiver down my spine as we spooned apricots out of a tin to keep up our energy levels, and offered some to our companion, who refused, pointing to his liquid refreshment.

In the circumstances we had already decided to abandon the assault on the summit on account of safety. All our energies were now concentrated on a secure retreat. For about the tenth time I looked outside the door and was suddenly rewarded with a completely magical sight. Snow had stopped falling and the cloud cover had dropped into the valleys, leaving us perched above it, gazing into a white foamy sea, with the highest peaks like islands amongst it. Another layer of cloud hovered above us obscuring the tip of Antelao, leaving us sandwiched between the layers, watching, as the boiling clouds below continually washed the shore of surreal, mythical islands.

We decided to make use of this window in the weather to start back down the mountain and even managed to galvanize our boozy friend into action, but here another impending catastrophe immediately presented itself. The ridge was now well snow covered after the storm and while we were proceeding carefully, all of us roped together and moving in unison, our third party member decided to speed things up by glissading on the seat of his trousers! We shouted on him to stop and reined him in as he shot past us, plunging our axes into the snow and chugging forcefully on the rope before he pulled us all over the edge. Changing places in line we carried on until we cleared the snow and as the clouds below lifted we had another stunning view, this time right up the valley far below to the North, all the way from St Vito to Cortina. The day had not been entirely wasted after all.

147

Looking back towards the heights of Antelao we saw that the top was still cloud capped and more bad weather seemed to be rolling in from the south west, making us realize we had definitely made the right decision to descend. We quickened our pace to get off the ridge before the new weather front arrived, and having located the path down the cliff we started the treacherous descent, keeping the Italian safe between us. Despite his consumption of spirits during the day he was surprisingly sure footed and athletic, and after our final scree run down the valley to the hut, he thanked us graciously, making us feel like heels, but knowing we had learned a lesson. Be firm – and we had not been firm enough!

We packed up our belongings and made ready to start down the track to St Vito in the late afternoon, and having reached it we began hitching up the road to Cortina, being overjoyed when the first vehicle that stopped belonged to the Dutch couple camped next to us. What a stroke of luck at the end of the day.

Our second Dolomite holiday was now drawing to a close, but in two years time we had something else in mind. The year after our marriage, we were looking to go to Zermatt and Chamonix, places I had read about in books of the Alps. Zermatt in particular was a long held dream, as that was where the Matterhorn was situated, the iconic mountain that featured so often in advertisements, particularly on chocolate box lids, which is where I'd first seen it. The chocolates had appeared in one of my school staffrooms in Glasgow at the end of a term, and everyone had dived in during the morning coffee break. When it was my turn to indulge I was more interested in the box, which had an amazing colour photo of the Matterhorn on the lid. I asked the staff not to throw out the box and when the chocolates were finished I took it home with me. For years it became my jewellery casket on the dressing table – not that I was a jewellery person, but I had wood and bead necklaces, popular in the sixties, and silver steel brooches I'd bought in the Dolomites, of climbing boots, ice axes, ropes and edelweiss.

I read any books I could find on the Matterhorn and studied Edward

Whymper's various attempts, including his successful one in 1865, which marked the first time it had been climbed. In 1965, which was the centenary of this achievement, a re-enactment was televised by the BBC. It took place on the famous Hornli Ridge, which had been Whymper's chosen ascent, complete with an experienced climbing team and camera crew. I'd watched it avidly on our black and white TV in Pitlochry and I came to the conclusion that it might even be doable by myself and a companion some day! What I didn't realise at the time of course was that due to the extreme gradient and the standard of filming expertise at the time, the shots were foreshortened, turning the ridge into what resembled a steep scramble, without any realistic representation of the daunting exposure involved.

It became my ambition to attain the summit of this spectacular pyramid in the Alps and John and I were hoping to accomplish this in 1969 - before we moved north to Sutherland - before we had kids and dogs - and before we felt obliged to settle down like normal people - without thinking up arduous and impractical goals.

# PART 5: THE ALPS – ZERMATT & CHAMONIX 1969

# 1

# ZERMATT AND THE METTELHORN

When we left for the Alps in July 1969 the intention was to spend three to four weeks between Zermatt and Chamonix, depending on how long we could make our finances last. During this time we hoped to consider an ascent of Monte Rosa, the highest peak in the Zermatt area, and also to explore the Hornli Ridge on the Matterhorn which was the most iconic. In Chamonix we wanted to investigate Mont Blanc, the highest mountain in the Alpine chain, but other than that there was no particular plan until we arrived there and reviewed the situation. It was one thing to have visions and a plan, but accomplishing this was another matter and like all ambitious projects success was not guaranteed.

In 1967 we'd had problems fixing up last minute insurance for mountaineering, but this year we managed to get a package with the Ramblers Association in Finchley Road in London, for the much lesser price of £4. We were astonished at such a low charge for tackling the Matterhorn, but were assured it would be adequate. In fact we wondered later if the man behind the desk actually knew what an ascent of the Matterhorn entailed?!

We travelled to the Alps via Cross Channel Ferry to Calais, followed by trans-continental trains to Paris and Brigue in Switzerland, where we alighted to catch the train on the cog railway up the steep valley to Zermatt. In 1969 no motorised transport was allowed in the streets of Zermatt, except for electric milk floats. On arrival at the terminus a fleet of horse drawn cabs were to be seen in the yard outside, ready to convey foreign tourists and their luggage to hotels, while the walking and mountaineering fraternity shouldered their packs and made off on foot. As we belonged to this group we decided to head up the main street too, on a mission to explore and catch sight of some of our objectives.

The Matterhorn was visible almost at once, towering up from the rear of the chalet town. We stopped in our tracks dumbfounded. It seemed to fill the sky with giant and perpendicular proportions, nothing like my alluring snow covered pyramid from the chocolate box, softened with a ring of Alpine flowers. "Is that it?" I said to John, stating the obvious, with unanswered questions flooding my brain. Who were we to think we could scale such a formidable giant? We had completely underestimated the difficulties that would be involved in tackling such a monster. I tried to pick out the Hornli Ridge that I'd seen on TV, which had looked doable in the foreshortened photography of the time, but what I now saw in reality looked like an ice-sheathed, vertical stairway to hell, with imminent disaster lurking on every rung. The Queen of the Alps was certainly majestic, but beneath the charm lurked a deadly sting for the unprepared!

John didn't say much, except, "Let's get a meal, book accommodation and make an acclimatization plan."

The town had a plentiful supply of hotels, restaurants and bars, and in the main street, intermingling with the tourists, were climbers and guides, distinguishable by their cord or leather breeches, red socks, stout boots, alpenstocks and coils of rope. We chose a restaurant near the top of the street and took our German phrase books out ready to order a meal, but the waitress was American, so there was no need. In fact I was disappointed that there was such a big American influence in the town, which I had not expected – capped by a musician tuning up with guitar, singing country western songs from Nashville in English! I had anticipated accordions, Tyrolean hats, slapping of leather breeches and yodelling at the very least, alias 'Seven Brides for Seven Brothers', but apparently, as with kilts and bagpipes in Scotland, they keep all that for special occasions. I considered broaching the subject of non-traditional entertainment to the management, but on second thoughts decided it was best not to make a scene.

After leaving the restaurant we bought a detailed map of the area in the information office and enquired about accommodation for walkers and climbers. In this respect we were directed to the Bahnhof, which was an imposing building several storeys high, opposite the railway station. Inside however, it was not quite so flush, although it had various classes of accommodation, ranging from double and twin rooms to youth hostel bunks in dormitories. It was fully self-catering with a spacious kitchen occupying most of the basement, decorated with full size posters of the nearby Gornergrat narrow gauge railway. Closer inspection revealed them to be covering plasterwork discrepancies below!

We decided to splash out and book a double room with luxurious duvets. Such bed coverings had not quite caught on yet in Britain, but we decided to make enquiries when we returned and purchase one, which would be so much easier than three heavy, old fashioned blankets. The main reason for our extravagance was because the bunk rooms were strictly either male or female, even for married couples like ourselves!

The proprietor of the establishment whom we referred to as 'madame' was a tartar for discipline and a stickler for rules. She was continually checking up on people in the kitchen, watching out for any dirty dishes and pans left in the sinks. We were not too sure how long we would stay as the idea was actually to go up to the huts above the glacier once we were organised.

In the evening we revised our impressive mountaineering plans and decided to go for a lower peak first in view of the need to get acclimatized. We located one on the map at 11,173 feet called the Mettelhorn, but as we were already situated at around five and a half thousand feet in Zermatt this only left about the same again to be ascended, and it was more than three thousand feet lower than the lofty Matterhorn, with similar sounding name, but considerably less technical difficulty and exposure.

While we were breakfasting in the Bahnhof kitchen early next morning, madame appeared with a basket of laundry, so we asked her advice on the best approach to the Mettelhorn. This was apparently to turn right at the local bakery in the main street, then follow the path to the Alterhaupt Restaurant where we would find the track leading to our objective. However, it wasn't quite as simple as that.

We turned right at the appointed place and found that the path threaded a steeply sloping field of knee high grass, soaking with dew. On re-emerging from this, the path split into two with no indication as to where either fork was headed. We chose to go right again and after a short distance arrived in the backyard of an expansive chalet. Obviously we'd made a faux pas. Shades of Antelao!

We backtracked until we could see a long valley rising sharply ahead of us and a short distance away there was another path climbing over tufted grass towards it. We decided to take a short cut involving more wet grass and the steeper sections brought the hands into action too, resulting in wet sleeves as well as wet trouser legs.

Once we reached the main path up the valley the situation improved with less vegetation and a well trodden stony track that zig-zagged into a tight gorge leading to the Alterhaupt Restaurant. Unfortunately this seemed to be closed for business. We decided to take a break outside it and watched an American who was sitting on the doorstep, filling rolls with what looked like uncooked bacon. At the head of the gorge we arrived at another building alluded to as the Trift Hotel, but it was very definitely defunct and had been for some time. Despite its ruinous condition however one of the rooms appeared to be in use as a doss by climbers. There were some old wooden chairs in it so we sat down and had a snack, while a party of Germans brewed up coffee on a primus and drank it out of saucepans.

The altitude was now beginning to take its toll and there was still some considerable distance to go. The path wound its way up onto a high shoulder where we hit the snowline and found ourselves crossing what looked like a permanent snow field. In addition, a wind was whipping up, blowing loose material around and adding to the chill factor. We had been told that the climb from Zermatt could take around five hours, but by the time we'd crossed more successive snow and ice fields, circumnavigated a peak of lesser height which lay between us and the main summit, and finally laboured up the last more exposed slope to the top of our objective, almost seven hours had passed.

As we peered gingerly over the summit cone in a strengthening ice cold wind we had a hazy view down sheer cliffs towards Zermatt, where the buildings appeared like a sprinkling of celestial dots from another world as they faded into the enclosing mist. I felt completely exhausted and could hardly keep my feet when the strongest gusts descended, during which my shades flew off and disappeared down the slope into the abyss, while at the same time John lost a glove. Much as we wanted to linger on the summit and take photos after all that effort, it was useless because we couldn't hold the camera steady and we thought we'd better retrace our steps to the lower slopes before we got frost bitten. Early evening was already approaching and we wanted to get back to Zermatt before dark. My nose was also starting to feel like an icicle and John said he couldn't feel his fingers. Summer holiday indeed!

Once we lost height and the wind dropped it was much warmer and our return to the valley far below was spectacular, as we glissaded down the snow slopes we'd toiled up earlier and jogged back down the stony path through the gorge, accomplishing the descent in two and a half hours.

Back in town in the late evening we thought we deserved a decent meal, so we booked one at the Derby Hotel, after leaving our gear at the Bahnhof and freshening up.

The following day was spent exploring Zermatt and making preparations to go up to the high glacier at the foot of Monte Rosa, where there was a mountain hut for those considering ascents of some of the most prestigious peaks in the area. Our objective was another four thousand feet higher than the Mettelhorn, which would be no mean feat to achieve. Well there was nothing like having a grand plan in the impetuousness of youth. Monte Rosa was also higher but less exposed and perpendicular than the Matterhorn, which was to be our final objective in Zermatt.

We had no idea of the route to the summit of Monte Rosa and knew little of the avalanche danger, but we presumed we might get advice at the hut, although we were not going to fall into the trap we'd inadvertently walked into on Antelao in the Dolomites two years earlier. We were explorers and we were going to give the region's highest peak a go ourselves!

During our day in Zermatt we decided to look round the local museum which detailed early ascents of the Matterhorn and other less fruitful ones, along with information about well known former local guides and their clients. It turned out to be an unexpectedly spine chilling tour with graphic images of historical disasters, many of them on the Hornli Ridge which we had in mind to tackle! There were oil paintings depicting corpses in torn clothing, minus limbs, hanging from frayed, broken ropes over sheer ice walls, and detailed accounts in several languages describing how these fatalities had occurred, including the demise of some of the most respected pioneer men and their guides of the time.

We shivered at these gruesome disclosures. What were we thinking of, tackling these horrendously dicey routes where so many better equipped and more knowledgeable mountaineers than ourselves had perished? When we left the museum we walked solemnly through the graveyard, looking sadly at the graves of the 19th century climbers and respected local guides, amongst whom were renowned members of the Taugwalder family from Zermatt, before deciding to cheer ourselves up with a lunch time drink in one of the local bars.

Well we didn't have to do any of these things, but we were certainly going up to the glaciers the next day for a look at the wider area, including Monte Rosa, and also a glance towards the Matterhorn from a different angle, across the massive Gorner Glacier.

# 2

# MONTE ROSA

The following morning saw us queuing with our packs for the Gornergrat mountain railway which was next door to the Bahnhof and would take us up to the glaciers high above the town on route for Monte Rosa. It climbed steeply up the slopes to the south east of Zermatt, onto an exposed ridge opposite a stunning panorama of the most iconic snow clad peaks of the region, while below lay the dazzling, white expanse of the Gorner Glacier, glistening in the morning sun. We alighted from the train at the Rotboden halt, which was at the beginning of the ridge. It was the climbers' stop for access to Monte Rosa and Lyskamm, amongst other challenging tops nearby, while tourists travelling on the train carried on to the terminus where there was an impressive stone built hotel, with viewing terraces, meals and accommodation.

A path ran down from Rotboden to the edge of the glacier, where there was a beaten track across the ice, marked by wooden posts, denoting a relatively safe crossing to the other side and access to the Monte Rosa Hut, said to be a two hour walk. It was our first experience of crossing a glacier and involved stepping over a number of narrow slit like crevasses on route. Two glaciers met below Monte Rosa, the Gorner and the Grenz and where they joined forces we had to scramble over a massive heap of moraine slag, at the side of which were deep green pools of icy melt water. On the far side of the glaciers we had to climb up to the hut over ice-free, sun-baked slopes of rubble and boulders. This was hot work with continual glare overhead, but our laborious slog was enlivened by the appearance of dozens of furry creatures about the size of a small rabbit with short tails that stood up like a brush. They were surprisingly tame and obligingly posed for photographs. We later discovered they were marmots, which were prevalent in the Alps, as common as the rabbits that scampered on the dunes in Britain.

When we arrived at the hut which was close to the edge of the snowline we saw that it was similar to the Dolomite mountain huts, being stone built, several storeys high, with a fenced terrace to the front, and rows of identical windows with red shutters, decidedly more aesthetic than the Galassi Hut on Antelao. How they built these palatial mansions in such remote, inhospitable places beggared belief, but we presumed that most of the materials were dropped by helicopter. The hut supplied cooked meals, washing facilities and rooms with mattresses on the floor for climbers. The toilets however were outside in contrast to our experience in the Dolomites. They were housed in three cubicles across an area of hard pan ground opposite the hut and perched right above the glacier. Each cubicle had a wooden door in two halves like a horse box and inside was a bench seat. The relevant aperture looked down on the glacier below which discouraged lingering in windy weather, while toilet paper was supplied by sheets of newsprint suspended from a nail on the wall. As the doors didn't lock you had to be ready to grab them from inside if anyone should suddenly chance to hoist them open!

The hut keeper had a smattering of English, but he understood that we were interested in an ascent of Monte Rosa and imparted the information that if this was the case we should be aware that a start would have to be made at 2am, in order to climb above the lower snow slopes before the avalanches started to come down around midday. We digested this news with a tinge of apprehension, but we were still prepared to give it a go, until a heavy snowstorm came on in the evening. Flakes like saucers were floating down by 7 o'clock and the hut keeper said that it might not be possible to make an ascent. If this was the case he wouldn't waken us as was customary and we would have to wait till the following day.

The situation was not looking at all promising and there was an eerie solitude in the hut that night as not many people were about. Nevertheless we retired early in case we were called.

Overnight I dreamed I was about to fall into a crevasse and every time I wakened I fumbled for my torch to see the time. Two o'clock came and went without a call, for which I had to admit I was relieved after the previous evening's unexpected wintry weather.

In the morning we breakfasted at 9 o'clock with the sun now blazing down and the overnight snow rapidly melting. We decided not to waste the day, so spent our time reconnoitring the slopes above the hut and taking photographs of each other with the Matterhorn in the background. The view across the glaciers in front of the hut was stunning and we spent hours identifying points on the Hornli Ridge that we might be able to reach in a few days' time. Despite Monte Rosa's superior height the Matterhorn was the Queen of them all, resplendent and unique in isolation, standing out from its more prosaic neighbours, its symbolic shape triumphantly piercing the sky - captivating climbers with its enduring charm - luring them forwards and upwards - 'try me if you dare'. I felt a ripple of excitement, tinged with a slight foreboding at the thought, but first of all we had our ascent of Monte Rosa to consider.

We climbed a fair distance towards it that afternoon, prospecting the route, until we heard from various directions the rattle of stonefalls and the eerie explosions of collapsing seracs, along with constant creaking from the glacier below as it inched its way slowly down the valley. We were also wary of the sudden afternoon avalanches as described by the hut warden, and mindful of this danger we decided to make our way back downhill.

There had seemed to be no definite route or emblazoned trail towards the summit of Monte Rosa and there were various obstacles in between expansive snowfields, gradually rising in gradient.

It would be a long grind at high altitude with the summit more elusive than it seemed – like many Scottish hills when one thought the top was just over the next shoulder, only to find it was not. In view of sun glare on exposed facial projections, we had developed a method of dealing with this. In addition to lashings of glacier cream, we had a piece of cardboard, folded in half and sellotaped to our goggles to protect the nose from severe sunburn. Mine was already blistered and peeling. We began to see other climbers adopting the same method, but it wasn't entirely satisfactory, because if you didn't secure it sufficiently and a wind blew up, it would either flap in front of the eyes, rendering one unable to see, or it would fly off altogether and disappear!

In the late afternoon there were fresh arrivals at the hut, mostly French and German men, and all of them were apparently planning an ascent of Monte Rosa the following day. We gravitated towards the French and sat with them on the terrace, talking in English. We had bought a postcard of the mountain earlier from the hut keeper's supplies and the guys obligingly drew out the normal route of ascent on it for us, saying that if we started out early just behind them, we would be able to follow their footsteps. This lifted our morale and the weather was said to be improving, so we retired early in view of the 2am start.

This time there was no hitch and we were wakened by the warden knocking loudly on the dormitory doors. The Germans had already left while we were getting our equipment together and drinking our coffee in gaslight, and the French left just in front of us.

It was still dark when we began trudging through the snow above the hut, necessitating the use of our head torches. The Germans were out of sight, but to begin with we could dimly make out the torch beams of the French a short distance ahead. This didn't last long however, as the all-male party were super fit and experienced, definitely on a mission, with few stops for snacking, photographing images or clarifying the route. We did all these things in addition to nose-blowing and reattaching our cardboard strips, but more significantly we were revelling in the rising of the Alpine dawn, which was a brilliant spectacle not to be missed, including a striking silhouette of the Matterhorn against the glacier.

We attempted to follow in the footsteps of the French, but it wasn't that easy as spindrift blowing along the ground was filling them up. It was magically quiet being on the mountain so early in the morning, but the higher we climbed the harder it was becoming to keep up a brisk pace.

We had started out from the hut at a height of about nine thousand feet and we were now nearing twelve, higher than we'd ever climbed before. The altitude was beginning to tell and as the dawn gave way to daylight and the sun climbed into the sky above us we were being roasted and scorched unmercifully, despite all the snow underfoot. Occasionally we caught sight of dots on the horizon, but we were not sure whether it was the Germans or the French and sometimes we thought it was just a trick of the light or a speck of dirt on our goggles.

Cols and seracs were appearing ahead and we were slightly anxious about the impending avalanche danger and the need to keep going. Our pace had slowed considerably. I felt I was frying up under the sun and at the same time I had increasing difficulty in breathing and getting enough energy to move forward and upward. We were approaching thirteen thousand feet, but there was still a long way to go. The horizon looked a million miles away with obstacles in between that swam in and out of focus. I should have acquired a hat with a brim like other Alpinists I had seen. That might have helped. Other niggling worries started to come into my mind at this point too – like the possibilities of sunstroke, severe glacier burns, snow blindness or altitude sickness. I'd had sunstroke once before, when I was seven years old, after lying for an extensive period on a beach of white sand in Cornwall and I didn't want to repeat the experience. It could ruin our attempt on the Matterhorn?

We stopped to reconsider our position and options and decided that in the circumstances retreat was the best decision. We would also have to be quick to beat the avalanche danger. Our speed accelerated as we descended, and along with this came increased energy levels and a lifting of morale. There was no disgrace in having failed to reach the summit. We were on a learning curve for this type of terrain and we knew that it was certainly not technical difficulty that had beaten us. It was lack of sufficient acclimatization. We hoped to be better prepared for the Matterhorn.

It was still early afternoon when we regained the back door of the hut and collapsed into the welcoming cool shade of the interior. We had been on the mountain for nearly twelve hours and in view of our exertions we made straight for the dining room and ordered lunch before repairing to the dormitory for an afternoon kip. I couldn't remember ever having been so pleased to find respite from strong relentless sunlight! We slept for most of the afternoon and in the evening we got up and went downstairs to the dining room for another meal, followed by observations of the sunset from the terrace outside and chat with the men returned from the tops.

In the morning we ordered cheese toast for breakfast, but it was burnt black on one side, soggy in the middle and a thick coating of strong tasting cheese with the consistency of putty was plastered on top. Not to be recommended! After that sinker we paid our bill and set off back to Zermatt, beginning with the long trek across the glaciers, followed by the train from Rotboden.

On our arrival we went straight to Leo Perrens Supermarket to get some provisions before returning to the Bahnhof. We'd been planning a snack in the kitchen, but an unpleasant, unidentifiable smell there made us change our minds and take our fare up to the double bedroom we'd been allocated. As snacking in the bedrooms was frowned upon we took care not to drop peach stones in the waste paper basket and leave crumbs on the carpet, but unfortunately I spoiled things by leaving a stain of bramble jam on the dressing table mat. My efforts to remove it with a sponge and nailbrush only spread the stain further, so eventually I put an ash tray on top of it and hoped for the best.

In the evening we took advantage of hot water supplies to do some washing, write postcards home and go out for a meal of roast chicken at the Derby, which was fast becoming our favourite restaurant in Zermatt.

We had intended having a lazy couple of days in the town to recuperate from our Monte Rosa exertions, before attempting the Matterhorn, but an unexpected announcement first thing next morning left us bristling with annoyance. Nor was it anything to do with the bramble jam on the dressing table mat!

A loud rat-a-tat on the bedroom door announced the arrival of a German chamber maid who told us in stilted English that our room was booked that night and we would have to move to the dormitories in the attic. We stared at her in disbelief before Madame appeared on the scene and with a slight apology for the inconvenience, confirmed the fact that we would have to move upstairs, and as per the rules of the establishment it would be separate dorms. We were decidedly unchuffed, but could do nothing about it, except refuse and find ourselves in the street without accommodation. As it was the height of the holiday season and Zermatt was chock a block, we'd been lucky to get into the Bahnhof in the first place.

Swearing under our breath we lugged our belongings up to the attic and found the dorms. Mine had four pairs of bunks in a small cramped room, and was piled with possessions and bags strewn about the floor. I was speechless as I surveyed the room from the doorway and an American lounging on one of the bottom bunks declared that the room was full. At this point Madame appeared behind me and declared this was not the case. So and so had paid their bill that morning and left. I was thankful that we were moving out the next day to a hut on the Matterhorn.

This was to be a rest day exploring the outskirts of Zermatt and recuperating from our overdose of sun on Monte Rosa. In the afternoon we returned to the Bahnhof to read books in the kitchen, which was now preferable to the dormitory, but it wasn't long before Madame arrived with the proverbial bucket of paste and fresh posters for cover up jobs, until the task was interrupted by a gentleman demanding a lock for the shower room.

Three English lads arrived shortly after and shared our table in the kitchen for a meal of fried spam and spaghetti. We had a great chat with them as they were enthusiastic walkers and climbers with aspirations to tackle the Matterhorn. Our conversation continued on the terrace outside the front door, then when two guys appeared marching up the street in climbing attire, check shirts and red socks, our companions said, "There's the two men that are going to tackle the North Face of the Matterhorn tomorrow." Wow! We were impressed. All eyes followed them as they disappeared up the street, then when it was suggested we go out for a drink at one of the bars with outside seating we jumped up immediately.

I dashed up to the dormitory to fetch my jacket, but a shock greeted my arrival there. Someone was sleeping in the bed I'd been told was free and my pack had been added to a pile on the one next to it! Madame was conveniently unavailable and waking up the offending individual was only going to lead to an argument. I decided to leave it until we returned from the pub.

I hurried back down the stairs to join John and our three companions and we set off into the area known as the old town of Zermatt, looking for a pub with character and cheap beer. We found the ideal place, with rustic tables and benches in the street, and better still our two North Wall men were sitting at one of them. As we approached their table they moved up the bench and invited John and I to join them, while our other friends fetched beer crates from the yard and sat opposite us. We were now a party of seven, all British, and with a similar aim to climb the Matterhorn. The North Wall pair introduced themselves as Ron and Pete and said they had climbed the Matterhorn before, but not by the North Face, which would be a much more challenging route. As far as I could see, craning my neck to the horizon, any route on the Matterhorn was going to be challenging!

We had a grand night of swapping stories, and drinks were ordered by shouting through an open window. However, in view of climbing the following day up to the Hornli Hut, we left to return to the Bahnhof at 10pm. When I opened the door of the dormitory I saw that the room was crowded and some occupants were already sleeping. The remaining two empty bunks were strewn with bags and possessions, indicating that they were claimed and my pack that I'd slung onto one of the supposedly vacant bunks earlier was now on the floor. This was not on. With a sigh of resignation I pulled out my sleeping bag and threw it up onto the top bunk not yet occupied, shifting items lying there to the remaining unoccupied bunk underneath. Hoping for the best I lay back, but I felt something underneath the pillow and found a pair of spectacles and a book. This wasn't looking good. Madame had no right to tell me that a bunk was free in this room. She'd told me a lie. Well it was first come, first served I thought peevishly as I dropped the book and specs onto the bunk underneath, which already had a pair of pyjamas on top of the pillow. I shut my eyes and waited with baited breath to see what happened next.

I was soon to find out. The door opened five minutes later and in the darkness I heard someone coming in and rummaging about on the bunk below me. There were some hefty sighs and muttered expletives as I heard her throwing all the possessions heaped on the bunk onto the floor, before climbing in and bedding down. All the beds were now occupied so there were bound to be fireworks if anyone else appeared. There was not long to wait.

An American threw open the door - on popped the light and there was an electrifying pause while she was obviously assessing the situation. I tried to keep my eyes squeezed shut, waiting on the outburst that was sure to follow.

"Well I never!" came the shrill exclamation, "Someone's pinched my bed!"

I quailed and snuck down further beneath the covers. What was going to happen now?

Suddenly everyone was awake, raised on one elbow, and adding their pennyworth to a heated discussion on the mad disorganisation of the dormitories. It being too late to contact the management with our complaints we decided to take matters into our own hands, shovelled the pairs of bunks together and made room for one extra. The plan was to do battle in the morning, but when morning came the drama seemed to dissipate slightly as most occupants packed up early and left.

John and I however were planning to hang around until the afternoon, when we thought it would be cooler trudging up the lower slopes of the Matterhorn to the hut, so with this in mind there would be no point in antagonising Madame and getting thrown out before we were ready to go, especially since she'd said we could leave excess luggage in the ski room until we left the area.

We bought tinned sausages, potatoes and frozen pimentos for a late lunch and took them back to the Bahnhof kitchen, but no sooner had we spread everything out when Madame arrived with her paste bucket and brush. Being surprised that we were still on the premises after paying our bill she asked us what our plans were, and when I said we were hoping to climb the Matterhorn she was horrified! "No! No!" she cried throwing her paste brush into the bucket with a splash. "It is very dangerous. Three were killed on it already this week. The British tourist – they think they can come to Zermatt and do everything!!"

We flinched in annoyance. Who did she think she was dictating to us like that, making out we were a couple of amateurs. Well maybe we were in some ways, particularly concerning Alpinism, but we were not necessarily going to hold out for the summit at all costs. We did have a grain of sense, but there was no harm in having a look and exploring the Hornli Ridge as far as we dared – and she was certainly not going to stop us.

We ate our lunch smouldering and threw the unappetising, overripe pimentos into the garbage can, then we shouldered our packs and left, heading for the cable car which would take us as far as the Schwarzsee Hotel, cutting the distance we had to walk to the Hornli Hut. We were both excited and slightly apprehensive about the demanding undertaking we were planning.

# 3

# THE MATTERHORN

When we arrived at the cable car station for Schwarzsee at the far end of Zermatt we were in for another setback. The station had closed for the day and would not be re-opening until the following morning. We were stunned at this revelation and annoyed with ourselves for not making relative enquiries into the operating times, which now left us with the alternative of walking or going back to the Bahnhof.

"We're not going back, that's for sure," I said, "to hear Madame crow, 'You didn't get very far!'"

It was unanimously decided to walk up to Schwarzsee and maybe spend the night there, before continuing to the Hornli Hut in the morning. This would involve three thousand feet of climbing and would probably take us until evening, so there would be no point in going on to the Hornli Hut at that time with fading light restricting good photo opportunities and disguising possible path obstacles too.

The change of plan took the edge off our enthusiasm as we began the uphill slog through the forest to Schwarzee, groaning under our heavy packs and the sun still grilling overhead. On the way we met a few climbers descending who said that we might still make the Hornli Hut that night, but it was a good five hours walk! We thanked them politely for this information, declining to mention that we had already come to a decision to stop at Schwarzsee.

It wasn't long after that when we reached the halfway cable car station called Furi, where we stopped for a rest and to admire the spellbinding view opening out in front of us as we cleared the forest. From this point the path became much steeper as it twisted upwards towards our objective and as we ploughed on the sky began to take on the dusky tinge of early evening with the sun slowly disappearing, leaving us in a silent, shadowy world as we reached the hotel.

During the day the establishment and its terraces facing the Matterhorn were apparently a hive of activity, with tourists training telescopes on the Hornli Ridge and feasting on the hotel's culinary delicacies, but when we arrived the terrace was empty. Day trippers had descended in the last cable car and apart from some illuminated windows in the hotel, there was no other sign of activity. The building was situated a stone's throw from the cable car station and had obviously been built for the burgeoning tourist trade that the Matterhorn had attracted. It looked palatial and expensive, but it didn't prevent us from walking in the front door to the reception hall to make enquiries.

The first task was to make our request understood to the girl behind the desk who appeared to have limited English. However, I rustled up my German acquired at the tourist night class in Glasgow and along with a quick check in my phrase book we met with success. The receptionist smiled broadly and led us upstairs to a commodious dormitory which was empty and cost six francs per night. We thought that was a snip for such swell lodgings and accepted it right away.

In the morning we had bacon and eggs in the cafeteria which was a real treat, but afterwards while packing up John announced he'd lost his camera, which looked set to delay us as he searched the dormitory, the cafeteria and the terrace outside, where we'd paused to look at the landscape the previous night. We dug out our phrase books again and looked up some intelligent German for 'Have you found a camera?' then having pieced together a sentence that I thought would convey the general idea I approached the receptionist and repeated it to her.

" Oh ya!" she exclaimed, and diving under the counter at the desk she produced the camera, which was a huge relief.

The hike up to the Hornli Hut was both spectacular and sweltering under the glare of the sun at high altitude, as we were now climbing from around eight and a half thousand feet to nearly eleven and crossing the snowline. Abundant photo opportunities also looked set to lengthen our trip and made us realise it had been a sensible decision to split our journey at Schwarzee to get maximum benefit. The fact that some of our photos turned out to be over exposed only came to light later, telling us we had to brush up on our camera settings for strong Alpine sunlight.

During our hike there were parts where the wind had swept the snow clear, while in other sheltered areas it was packed solid. At one stage we climbed a craggy knoll and near the top found a small stone shelter which could be used as respite from the sun, rain or wind. In our case it was sun. While we were there we watched an American nearby trying to photograph his teenage son, while repeatedly commenting, "If you put a smile on it would help!"

Gaining height above the knoll the path deteriorated until we were almost scrambling up part of the main ridge itself on a mixture of snow and ice, including a knife-edge section where we had the misfortune to meet another party approaching from the opposite direction. Two-way traffic in this situation was difficult, leaving both parties slithering dangerously close to the edge and plunging their axes into the snow for stability!

The steep final slope to the Hornli Hut was reached by a long series of zig-zags, said to number more than forty, and when we reached our objective we found it situated on the only flat square of land remaining, right underneath the start of the legendary climb on the Hornli Ridge. The renowned Alpine hut owned by the Swiss Alpine Club was a substantial stone construction jammed between the ridge and another building immediately in front, referred to as the Belvedere Hotel, which had a much shorter season and was only getting ready for opening while we were there. The hut on the other hand was the regular haunt of the Matterhorn guides and exuded character, history and charm. We felt honoured to be able to book a place there, where so many eminent pioneering mountaineers of past centuries had stayed, although the hut was said to have been renewed since the original one was built. Due to the premises being extremely busy we were told there would be a lengthy wait in the dining room for service and the guides were attended to first, but we were unconcerned, being content just to savour the atmosphere and chat to British climbers about their achievements and ambitions.

We enquired into the price of hiring a guide as it would be more likely to lead to success, but when we heard it was equivalent to £25 a head we knew we couldn't afford it. In those days £25 was a considerable amount of money and we were still hoping to go on to Chamonix. We would just have to try on our own and go as far as we dared.

Before dinner we sat on a low stone wall outside, bounding a limited terraced area where climbers were sorting through kit or fiddling with cameras. Behind us the Hornli Ridge soared and snaked into the sky in intimidating twists and turns, but photographs from this angle were foreshortened, taking away the awesome, perpendicular nature of the ascent. In front of us the ground fell away sharply in a long dizzy sweep for more than five thousand feet, down to Zermatt in the shadowy depths below, where the buildings were a mass of miniscule dots, like the spray from the flick of a paintbrush.

I was rapidly becoming completely overawed with the entire scene and wondered if we were being foolhardy in our ambitions. Then we saw Ron and Pete who had set off the day before us to tackle the North Face, but it transpired they were still waiting for suitable snow conditions and were preparing for a second attempt the following day. Ron joined us on the wall while Pete took photos of us, before an Irish party arrived, saying that they too were going to try the ridge unguided in the morning. Ron was something of a veteran Matterhorn climber and told us the story of a previous expedition he had made to the summit when their party was overtaken by bad weather on the way down and had to take shelter on the ridge overnight. When they had arrived at the hut the next morning the warden had accused them of using the Solvay Refuge, an emergency shelter for earmarked parties only, situated high on the final slopes, there being a fine imposed for transgressing the rules. We craned our necks to see if we could spot this exclusive hut, but it was too well camouflaged against the rock. The Matterhorn had become a serious business since Edward Whymper's first ascent in 1865. It was guarded by rules and regulations, accompanying aggro and debate.

We made enquiries from Ron about the best plan for our assault on the ridge and he said the biggest problem was the paying guided parties who set off early and continually knocked down loose stones as they scrambled upwards. Stone falls seemingly resulted from the kind of material that composed the ridge, being in part, loose slag, none of which was visible from a distance, or in the stunning photographs of the graceful white eminence, which adorned calendars, chocolate boxes and advertisements, world wide. Regarding these captivating images it was the proverbial case of 'better at a distance than close up'!

Seeing the ridge now from our position directly below, I realised where all this talk about loose slag was coming from. It was like a heap of grey rubble on top of rock, with the snow mostly confined to the faces and even that was patchy. Nevertheless the underlying disappointment did not deter us from our plans.

Our safest bet, Ron suggested was to let the guides get a reasonable distance ahead before we started the climb. We clocked this information with a growing sense of uneasiness. His parting comment as he left to return to the hut was, "By the way – my grandmother comes from Pitlochry!" I'd told him I used to live there, which led to another memory. Ben Smith, a Pitlochry hotelier had once told my mother that he had a nephew, Robin Smith, who was a fanatic climber, and that the aforementioned individual would make an excellent companion for her daughter. He had apparently promised to introduce us when his nephew returned from the Pamirs – only Robin never did return. He was killed during the expedition in 1962. Remembering all this was no confidence booster in view of our impending dicey venture the next day. My rosy picture of the Matterhorn was rapidly beginning to wilt around the edges.

Putting all this aside we quickly followed the boys into the hut's dining room to wait for our meal. The choice was spaghetti with cheese and tomato sauce or sardines. We knew we would have to wait to be served, but it was the Hornli Hut after all, and sharing it with the guides and their clients was a privilege. My friends and acquaintances back home would probably never come to a place such as this, nor on reflection would they want to be in such a place!

The suspense involved in waiting to try the ridge was electric. It was like being back stage in a theatre, waiting for your cue to dash out into the limelight and remember your lines in front of a large audience, whereas in this case, we mustn't slip up, or make a wrong move, only to be hurled down the sheer icy faces of the Matterhorn's cone, just like the oil paintings had graphically depicted in the museum in Zermatt – frayed ropes, rucksacks, bunnets and rocks all flying through the air – to say nothing of Madame's parting shot, "You British tourists – you think you can do everything!"

When I was young my greatest desire was to spend all day running across the mountains – but I couldn't help thinking that this was now a step too far!

After dinner I went outside again to stare up at the darkened, shadowy outline above me, before going in search of the outside toilets. They were in a shed at the far side of the building and there was no light. The floor was a sheet of ice. Having forgotten my torch I groped my way to one of the cubicles, feeling around to locate the seat, then I slipped, missed the pan and sat down unexpectedly on the floor, snecking my finger on the door catch in the process. I hauled myself off the floor, did the essentials quick, then hurried back to the hut, almost slipping again as I skated out the door. What hope for the Hornli Ridge if I couldn't even keep my feet on the level floor of the conveniences?

At night I hardly slept. Two o'clock came far too quickly and saw us up again drinking coffee in gaslight in the dining room. We let the guides go and waited again - then we put on our head torches, picked up our gear and our rope and crept out into the darkness.

The air was still and silent, and as we looked upwards along the line

171

of the ridge we could see pin pricks of light dancing above us. It was the guided parties and as we listened carefully we could hear the stones rattling faintly. The first part of the ridge was a rough steep scramble, deceptively easy, but the gradient soon increased. We could make out the ice and banks of snow glistening on the sheer faces to our left, but the ridge remained clear, apart from sheltered nooks and crannies where it hung on, packed tight. There was a mixture of black rock and buttresses on the ridge, along with shale and slag deposits on the ledges, interspersed with a ground down gravelly mixture, ripe for slipping on.

We roped up for safety in case of insecure rock, and watched our feet amongst the spoil on the ledges, as well as keeping a lookout for running missiles descending from above. The ridge decreased in breadth in some places, while in others it broadened out, with the climbing being of a reasonable to diff standard that would have been nothing in Glencoe, but on the Hornli Ridge was beset with intimidation, while the void below us was continually lengthening.

As the dawn spread across the mountain, it was impossible not to be aware of the exposure. The ridge was steepening too, and was looking more deadly ahead. After a more exacting pitch we found a stable pew above and reconsidered our position. I was already becoming gripped at the thought of reversing the pitch we had just done, possibly in darkness.

The early dawn was spreading so that it was unnecessary to use our head torches and the view was widening. Below was shocking emptiness and above there was rock and more rock. I tried not to think about the consequences of a fall, especially onto the face, which could terminate in oblivion amongst the creaking glaciers far below. As described in the museum in Zermatt such a slide would strip clothes and flesh, leaving only bones! I shuddered. It didn't bear thinking about. This was not the friendly Cairngorms of my youth, or the west coast of Scotland. This was the Alps, three or four times as high – beautiful - enticing - and the Matterhorn was the queen of them all, sheathed in its pristine robe of white when viewed from afar - magnificent but deadly! I thought of the deceiving chocolate box image and the impetuousness of youth - and said nothing.

Then we heard voices and two heads suddenly popped up from below, belonging to a couple of American gentlemen. They were also unguided and asked us if they could leave a pack where we were sitting while they took a look at the route ahead from above the buttress. We readily agreed, saying we were considering our options.

I wondered if John would be disappointed if we retreated, but he was the first to suggest it. We knew we had insufficient experience to complete this kind of venture and there were other factors - altitude, time, fatigue, bad weather scenarios - and more importantly, there would be difficulties involved passing the guides and their clients coming down if we continued. We'd had enough bother passing people proceeding in the opposite direction the previous day on an easier section of ridge, so what would it be like if we met them at the fixed ropes on vertical iced up rock below the summit?

We had already heard that many unguided parties failed to achieve their goal so it was no disgrace to turn back. It was the sensible thing to do in our position and even the Americans caught us up as we descended, having also decided to abandon the attempt. Maybe Madame at the Bahnhof had a point after all.

It was still only late morning when we arrived hack at the Hornli Hut and much to our surprise we found that Ron and Pete were back too. "Have you done the North face already?" I asked them.

"Heavens no!" came the quick reply. "The snow was too soft. We're trying again tomorrow, one last time before we go over to Chamonix."

"That's where we're headed," I told him. "Maybe see you there. Good luck on the face tomorrow – take care."

We collected the rest of our gear from the hut, paid our bill and set off back to Schwarzsee, covering the distance a great deal quicker than on our outward trip. We had a laugh on the way as we passed three men toiling up the path, all with different colours of cardboard sellotaped across the bridge of their nose. So my idea on Monte Rosa had not been so original after all! We were also distracted by the activities of a helicopter overhead, ferrying supplies to the Hornli hut and the hotel next door which was just opening for the season.

When we arrived at Schwartszee the terrace was packed with tourists who had come up for the day from Zermatt and were camera clicking excitedly, while others were looking through telescopes at the Matterhorn and the miniscule dots of climbers on the ridge. Maybe they had seen us earlier? Glancing around we noticed a cable car about to leave for Zermatt, so we dashed over and jumped aboard as it would save us a lot of time later on.

Once back in the bustle of the town our exploit on the Matterhorn above seemed to belong to another surreal world, as we quickly walked down to the Bahnhof to pick up the extra items of luggage we'd left in their ski room, hoping we didn't bump into Madame en route, who might ask how we'd got on! Having fortunately avoided that encounter we hurried over to the railway station opposite to see if there was still a late afternoon train for Visp. There was - and when we arrived at the foot of the valley we were fortunate to get another connection heading for Martigny near the French border - but there our luck ran out, because the last train that day for Chamonix had left, leaving us with two choices - hitchhiking or locating a room in Martigny. We decided to hitch.

Our first lift lasted about twenty minutes and took us uphill round a long, sharp bend into an expansive region of vine production. It was our only lift, because after that traffic was scarce and disinclined to stop. It was useless to start walking in growing dusk, in an area we were unacquainted with, besides which we were miles from Chamonix and exhausted after our early morning dawn exploits on the Matterhorn. There was only one solution to our predicament - a kip in the open amongst the vines in our plastic bivvy bag brought along for such emergencies.

I'd slept out before, on the slopes of Ben Vrackie at home, but I didn't really want to repeat the experience here. However, there was no alternative. We found a faint path leading into the vine plantation, so we followed it for a short distance uphill to a flattish area, where we pulled out our bivvy sheet. We spread it across the path and climbed inside, boots, jackets and all.

The night was interminable. It was cold and damp, with dew above and condensation within, hard and  uncomfortable below, while occasional screeches from night hunting birds had us jumping in alarm. We got very little sleep because the bag kept slipping down the slope and we had to constantly lever ourselves back into position on the flat! Nevertheless, I dozed eventually.

At the first light of dawn I was aware of voices coming down the path towards us and the appearance of two females who leapt over the top of our recumbent forms, giggling uncontrollably and repeating words that sounded like, "Scuzie – scuzie." We thought it was probably – 'Excuse me.'

In case this embarrassment happened again we got up and hitched back down the road to Martigny, before catching the morning train to Chamonix.

# 4

# CHAMONIX AND THE MER DE GLACE

I had read a lot about Chamonix. It was a Mecca for serious Alpinists and in the Golden Age of Mountaineering climbers had raced to put up new routes and make first ascents. We'd already visited the Italian and the Swiss Alps and at the other end of the chain was the French which was now our destination.

In Zermatt we had arrived with a plan of things we wanted to see and achieve, but in Chamonix we had no plan, partly because we didn't know exactly what was there and had no particular picture in mind. We knew that it housed Mont Blanc, the highest mountain in the Alps, but it didn't have the iconic image that the Matterhorn had achieved, mainly because it was tucked in at the back of outliers. Other notable eminences written about in books were in the area, but we had yet to identify the layout so the visit was to be something of a reconnaissance trip.

Zermatt had been compact and easy to navigate, and with the town having no motorised traffic, it had an old worldly feel to it. Chamonix on the other hand was spread eagled over a fairly wide valley. It was a much larger, busier and more commercialised than Zermatt, packed with traffic and coaches, creating noise and pollution, blowing out diesel fumes and blocking up thoroughfares. The pavements were crowded with international tourists, loitering in souvenir shops and queuing in restaurants and at first the climbers were lost in the crowd, or maybe they were all battling in the snow clad peaks high above us. We had been told to look out for the National Bar which was a watering hole for climbers and folk singers, particularly those from Britain, but initially our first priority was to secure accommodation.

We booked into the Hotel Beau Soleil et des Guides next door to the post office which was classed as a bed and breakfast, but there was no bacon and eggs in the dining room at 9 o'clock. The breakfast was continental and served in the bedrooms by a waiter who came upstairs with a tray of coffee, rolls and apricot jam in answer to a ring on the bell situated at the bedroom door. This situation did not lead to interaction with other guests and there was no visitors' lounge, so communication was dependant on us finding the National Bar.

On the afternoon of our arrival we bought some local maps and picked up brochures, then we went in search of the National Bar, but despite walking all over the town we drew a blank. The Alps rose steeply from either side of the valley, dressed in shades of green below, rising to buff colour then glittering snow piercing the sky above. We had to crane our necks to see the skyline and we presumed the highest point to the rear was Mont Blanc, although how this was approached we had no idea. At the present moment we were more concerned about locating the National Bar, but by evening it had still eluded us, so we returned unchuffed to the Beau Soleil and in view of our lack of sleep the previous night we decided to turn in and resume searching in the morning.

Despite falling asleep almost right away, I jumped awake again just after midnight on hearing a rumpus going on in the street. I sprang out of bed and looked out the window to see what was happening and caught sight of some well oiled individuals illuminated by street lamps across the road from our premises. They were brawling in a building site, sandwiched between a wheelbarrow and a cement mixer, with much shouting and physical activity. I watched for a few minutes transfixed, until they staggered off elsewhere and peace reigned. I was about to drop off to sleep again when another sound came floating upwards. It was Irish folk singing and I knew the song which was being sung in English.

Quickly I pulled on my jeans and sneaked downstairs to investigate. I opened the front door and looking towards the left I saw the National Bar on the opposite side of us from the Post Office, tucked into a corner. I couldn't believe it – and after searching the town all afternoon. Taking the stairs two at a time I hurried back to the bedroom and rousing John

177

I shouted that I'd just found the National Bar, declaring that we must go down immediately and join in the singing. The suggestion did not meet with agreement however. John was annoyed at being rudely awakened saying, "Don't be ridiculous. We can go tomorrow night!"

"Spoil sport!" I snapped grumpily, although I knew he had a point. It was 1 o'clock in the morning and we had too much sleep to make up.

The following day we widened our explorations of the town and the approach routes into the mountains, but the most eventful episode occurred in the evening in a local restaurant. We'd ordered Hors d'oeuvre selections for starters and the waiter duly arrived with a large platter, on which various different snippets were artistically arranged. He left it in the middle of our table and thinking they were all for us we halved the contents between us. However, when he returned to collect the platter and offer it to his next customers he pulled up short on discovering it was empty! We blushed, immediately realising we'd made a faux pas, but the waiter merely raised his eyebrows and swept the empty platter back towards the kitchen. The result of this was revealed during the substantial main course which we couldn't quite finish, but despite this the sweet course menu was so enticing that we couldn't resist a cream tart.

We were about to plunge into it when there was a shout from the other side of the restaurant. Customers were gathered round a black and white TV screen cheering and talking excitedly. We craned our necks to see what was going on and heard shouts of 'La Lune! La Lune!' and caught a glimpse of a fuzzy grey picture of the moon spread across the box, accompanied by a space suited figure. We realised with a start that we were watching man's first landing on the moon! There was more cheering and raising of glasses for a toast to this achievement in space exploration. Imagine seeing that in a French restaurant? We were gobsmacked.

Later in the evening we caught up with the clientele in the National Bar, where on this occasion there was no singing, but there were a number of climbers from Britain amongst the punters, some of whom were known to us. There were guys from Fort William, including John Grieve who later became the leader of the Glencoe Mountain Rescue Team and we were talking to them when I caught sight of Ron and Pete, our friends from Zermatt. "How did it go on the North Face?" I called over to them. They raised their glasses in a victory salute and told us they had been successful at the third attempt so we roundly congratulated them, although it didn't make us want to rush back to Zermatt and try the Hornli Ridge again! We also met Ian Clough, a notable climber of the period from England and we were shocked to hear the following year that he had been killed on Annapurna. It wasn't only the foolhardy that could have an accident in the mountains. The experienced were just as vulnerable, making us realise we'd done the sensible thing in retreating from the Hornli Ridge. We were not such fanatics that we had to push the boundaries and the older we became the more we felt disinclined to overstep the mark.

It was extremely hot and stuffy in Chamonix, so the next day we walked up into the mountains to cool off and explore the Mer de Glace, one of the best known glaciers in the Alps. It could be accessed by cog railway at considerable expense, but we chose to walk, threading several miles of steep forested land on a winding footpath to reach the Montenvers Hotel which overlooked the glacier and was situated near the terminus for the railway. From this spectacular vantage point there was an amazing view and nearby were various tourist attractions, including an Alpine zoo and a short cable car run onto the glacier itself, where visitors could inspect the ice grotto. At the hotel there was a viewing terrace with seating, waitress service for drinks and meals, and telescopes to identify important landmarks. We felt like proper tourists but we took advantage of all these things, except the cable car. Instead we walked down onto the ice over a rough footpath, before becoming tourists again, handing over our two franks for a squint into the ice grotto.

It was well worth the entry money to walk along the underground ice corridors, passing carved polar bears on route, until we arrived in a very chilly room with armchairs, tables, a piano and candles providing illumination. All these items were freshly carved each year and a photographer was waiting to capture visitors on camera and charging accordingly. We took our own photos!

Following this tour we went back up to the hotel and spent some time on the terrace identifying peaks on the far side of the glacier, which snaked high into the Alps. Amongst these were the Aiguille du Dru, Dent du Geant, les Grandes Jorasses etc, some having the appearance of bare rock spires. We decided they were quite out of our league so instead of tantalising ourselves with the impossible we went along to see the Alpine Zoo, admiring furry marmots and elegant chamois, along with a hoard of tourists. Having climbed three thousand feet above Chamonix to reach Montenvers we felt we had at least achieved something and were building up a picture of the geography of the area.

Nevertheless on returning to Chamonix John discovered that the sole of one of his boots was coming off, which left us with another predicament. We needed boots to climb and in view of the fact that we were running out of money this left us with two choices. One was to buy a new pair of boots in Chamonix where the selection was extensive and the price cheaper than in Britain, but the expenditure would curtail our holiday, while not buying them would limit our activities. After discussion we bought the boots and went home!

Back in our suburban Glasgow flat where all we could see from the windows were rows of grey tenements precipitated a feeling of depression. The exhilarating Alpine scenery was gone, but we decided to do something about this by constructing our own view of the Alps inside the flat. Within a bed recess space in the living room we built a fake window and bought a large Swiss Alpine mural from a DIY store in town, which we pasted along the wall. We edged it in wood panelling, top and bottom, including a window sill below and a pelmet at the top, behind which we concealed two strip lights, one for daylight and one for an evening sunset effect. I finished it off with net curtains at either side and after that we could happily sit in our living room and look out at the Alps, ignoring the real window at the other side with its uninspiring sea of tenement buildings!

Nevertheless we lasted barely another year in our flat in Cathcart Road, when it got to the point that we had to move north to the Highlands. John who had never lived anywhere else but Glasgow was keen to explore pastures new, while for me it was the pull of the wide open spaces and the hills to bring up children and get ourselves a collie dog.

When we left we didn't intend to go as far as we did, right into the Sutherland wilderness. The only thing I regretted leaving behind was our magical Alpine window. I could well imagine the people who bought our flat tearing it down and repapering the wall in loud, garish geometric patterns, popular in the early seventies! Oh well it was no concern of ours. We were going for the real mountain view in the Kyle of Sutherland.

When we later moved into Lairg on a more permanent basis our mountain holiday vision changed from the Alps to much further north, across the North Sea to the remote geothermal, living mountains of Iceland and east to the Viking lands and the mysterious Trolls of Norway, but that's another story.

# EPILOGUE

## RETURN TO CHAMONIX

It was eighteen years before we went back to the Alps, to Chamonix, during the October school holidays of 1987. We'd been invited to visit old friends who had moved to Paris and we jumped at the opportunity of also taking a trip down to the Alps to show them to our family, Heather aged sixteen and Iona, eleven. As Heather was shortly sitting her higher French exam it seemed like a good chance to practice her French as well. Our Parisian friends booked us accommodation in Chamonix for four nights, in a mountain chalet called Gite de la Montagne, which was situated in the forest not too far from the local rail station and the plan was to have a long weekend with our friends first, before travelling on south by train.

In Paris we did the sight seeing routine and the girls had a fabulous time. In fact they were so enthralled with the vibrant city life, exciting opportunities for things to do and see, not to mention Paris lit up at night like it was perpetual Christmas and handsome young French men whistling and waving to them on street corners – that come the day we had to leave for the Alps, they didn't want to go!

John and I were annoyed to say the least, but they were marched down to the Gare de Lyon railway station at the appointed time, protesting grumpily. I had to admit that the autumn weather had taken a downturn and was cold, grey and dreich, which didn't bode well for the Alps, contrasting with the last time we had been there in sizzling summer heat, with the high snow clad peaks etched against a deep blue sky. On this occasion it looked like we might not see the peaks at all.

It was to be a day of trains with our first one being the super fast TGV express to Annecy, said to be able to compete favourably with internal air travel between Paris and the Mediterranean coast. I'd booked four seats at a table situated in the middle of a carriage which turned out to be extremely tight for leg room, this being the first inconvenience. Our journey was scheduled to take four and a half hours and almost from the start the girls were squabbling and complaining, and playing footsie with the bags under the table that we'd been unable to squeeze into the rack above.

"You kicked me!"

"No I didn't - there's no room. The bags are in the way."

"Shut up and look out the window," I said.

"There's nothing to see. It's flat. The train's going too fast," was the moody reply as we zipped through stations whose names were impossible to read. Travelling alongside motorways we left cars standing, while livestock in the fields scampered hurriedly away and bushes doubled over sharply in the sudden blast of disturbed air pressure.

At Annecy we did a quick change into a local train for St Gervais that dawdled along by comparison and by the time we arrived there it was starting to grow dusk, just as the scenery was starting to become more interesting. Our third train to Chamonix was on the narrow gauge line which would take us right up into the heart of the mountains, to a height of over four thousand feet. By this time it was pitch dark with no view whatsoever and the girls were declaring they were cold as the single carriage train jogged, groaned and squeaked along, struggling with the gradient. It was packed with teenage school pupils doing their homework on their knees and the ten mile journey seemed to take for ever as rain intermittently streamed down the windows that rattled incessantly, while every so often gushing water could be heard thundering beneath the track. Groups of pupils constantly alighted at minor intervening stations and by the time we reached Chamonix there were only a handful left in addition to ourselves.

We had been told it was a twenty minute walk from the station to our accommodation and in the forecourt outside there was a map of the town on a billboard between two posts, so we stood and shivered in a stiff breeze, while we located our lodgings off the Bois du Bouchet road. La Montagne was marked in the forest off a track that led to the left from the Bois du Bouchet, so we started walking in that direction.

The buildings fronting the road soon came to an end and so did the street lighting, some of which didn't appear to be functioning at all, prompting us to rummage in our packs for torches. However the rain had stopped and the moon was out, illuminating the peaks high above us with their pristine white summits appearing to be floating in the sky above the dark forest below. "Look at that," I said to the girls with a rapturous surge of emotion. "Your first view of the Alps." But their reaction was completely unexpected.

"I'm cold," Heather said – while Iona gasped in shock and quickly looked away, holding tighter to my hand. I remembered that never in their lives had they seen anything that high, like a surreal white body floating in the sky, unattached to the earth below. I could see the word 'fiasco' firmly stamped against this holiday.

To make matters worse the torch battery was failing, but we managed to pick out our track leading into the forest on the opposite side of the road. A signpost pointed in the direction of Gite La Montagne so we set off into the forest hoping it wouldn't be too far.

Using both the light from the moon and our failing torch we soon found ourselves stepping over branches scattered on the ground and there was piles of other debris and larger bushy branches festooned with needles. Then all of a sudden we came upon a tree trunk right across the track and a jumble of black cables were dangling above it. Things were not looking good and when I shone the torch from side to side its feeble beam illuminated what looked like a marching army of stark, jagged, naked tree trunks of varying heights, with their tops ripped off and a remaining branch or two stretching what looked like a pleading, feeble hand towards us. We jumped and shivered with alarm, while Iona's grip on my hand tightened, then we noticed more cables - stout, black and insulated, weaving a pattern between the fallen trees, some at chest height and others trailing at ankle level. "Don't touch!" I shouted to the girls, fearing for electrocution, but John thought the power was off, with a storm having brought down the lines as the trees were torn apart. We knew nothing about any recent storm, not having been able to read the French newspapers over the weekend and there had been no disruption in Paris.

Things were not looking hopeful for the chalet, but we pushed on regardless as we had nowhere else to go - clambering, scrambling and tripping over mountains of debris and decapitated prickly, bushy heads smashed into the ground after their trunks had been slain. The remaining upstanding trees were groaning, squeaking and swaying overhead and we prayed that nothing else would fall while we walked underneath. It was a total nightmare!

After what seemed a good bit longer than twenty minutes we reached a stone wall and shortly after that we could just make out a faint outline of an enormous wood and stone built chalet, with weak emergency lighting glowing from several lower windows. We made our way to the front door, where there was a plaque that said 'La Montagne' and a notice marked 'entrée'. Pushing it open we found ourselves in a gloomy passage, where another notice told us that reception was upstairs. We clomped upwards on a long bare wood staircase, then another notice on the office door said, 'Attention! Moment!'

"It means the warden is away for a few minutes," Heather volunteered. So we backtracked and found a dimly lit kitchen on the ground floor. We dropped our packs and waited, saying nothing. Heather meanwhile went off to explore a path outside that went round the back of the chalet, but she was back sooner than I expected giggling uncontrollably.

"Well I'm glad you've found something to laugh about in this dire situation," I said, as she held up a sopping wet, dripping trouser leg. She explained that she'd fallen into a water butt, which I found difficult to comprehend, until I saw the set up in daylight. Several buckets and a large water butt had been reposing at the end of the path, gathering water

185

from the roof, and they were set into a large dug out hole at the corner of the building. "That'll teach you not to go exploring in the dark," I said, as she pulled dry trousers out her pack.

Shortly after that we heard footsteps on the stairs and a door banged above us. "That'll be the warden," I said and dashed up the stairs, but the woman behind the desk spoke nothing but French, and when I tried to explain our booking in English she just shook her head and carried on in French! I ran back down the stairs and grabbed Heather to come up and act as interpreter, and surprisingly, as soon as Heather started her attitude changed and she was a different woman, clapping her hands with enthusiasm and exclaiming, "Ah oui, oui," and handing over a key and our dormitory number. There was no point in trying to find out what had happened outside with our limited communication skills, although it was actually pretty obvious. I was just glad that the establishment was still up and running despite the lighting restrictions.

The following day when we looked out the front door we were astounded at what was revealed in daylight. The forest was devastated and all we could hear was the whine of chain saws and axes chopping and splintering, while the air was thickly laden with wood smoke. We had a quick breakfast in the kitchen before setting off to walk back into Chamonix, photographing the ravaged forest along the way, waving to the woodcutters, and scrambling over remaining piles of debris as the men fought to clear the track for supply vehicles, while others were attempting to speedily restore vital power supplies.

In town we headed for the tourist office where we were assured of an English speaking receptionist. In answer to our query about what had happened she said, "There was a very big storm at the weekend. Hundreds of trees are down and it will take a week to clear the railway track to Montenvers."

"Maybe we could walk up to the Mer de Glace?" I suggested.

"No! No!" she replied, waving her hands dismissively in the air. "You will not be able to walk up there this week. It is devastated up there and very dangerous."

We were decidedly taken aback by this information, because that had been the object of our holiday – to show the girls the magnificent glacier and the impressively grandiose, needle sharp peaks surrounding it.

"Is this normal October weather in the Alps?" I asked with a sigh.

"Oh no," she replied quickly. "If it was we wouldn't have a tree left standing."

Enquiries about other attractions in the area that might be available produced mainly negative replies. The swimming pool, ice rink and Alpine museum were closed, while all the cable cars bar one to the half way station, were shut down with electrical faults. It looked as if we were going to have a riveting time in Chamonix. We repaired to a café that sold creperie au chocolat to discuss the matter. Our Parisian friends had said that we would find Chamonix very busy and commercialised since our last visit in 1969, but this wasn't the case. Being October it was between climbing and skiing seasons. There were very few tourists about and coupled with the bad weather this had the effect of practically emptying the town.

We wandered through the streets and pointed out the Beau Soleil et des Guides where we had stayed previously and the National Bar next door, neither of which looked very active. Then we walked up to the one partially functioning cable car station on the other side of the valley to Mont Blanc, only to find it closed for lunch. Instead of waiting we bought some grocery supplies and went back to La Montagne to have a feast and plan what we could do for the next two days, given the present circumstances.

The first of these saw myself and the girls marching back to the cable car, while John elected to take a walk himself up to the next village of Les Praz. Our cable car experience took us to Plan Praz on the way to the Brevent, where we had a solitary ride in a small plastic cabin with eerie swooshing noises overhead, as we sailed serenely to a great height, bumping and shuddering over intervening pylons. The cars that passed us going down were all empty making us feel totally isolated, but the view from the half way station platform across the valley to Mont Blanc was spellbinding. Some cars were continuing to the upper station, but only for the conveyance of workmen to effect repairs.

When we returned to La Montagne we met up with John who said he'd climbed above Les Praz, right up to the cliffs below the Mer de Glace, and refuting what the receptionist at the tourist office had said, he didn't see why we shouldn't make it up there tomorrow, all the way to Montenvers. I had my doubts about the suggestion, but as an expensive coach trip through the Mont Blanc tunnel was the only alternative we could think up, with not much physical activity or particular view, I agreed to give it a go. The girls were less enthusiastic about the walk, but we talked them round.

The next day was dry but cloudy, so we set off on the path through the forest, heading for the Mer de Glace three thousand feet above us. Whether it was the same path that John and I had followed eighteen years ago I was not quite sure, as the amount of trees that had come down changed the perspective. We passed a few woodcutters and fires burning the debris, but no one tried to stop us as we tramped up hill, with glorious views opening up below, across the valley. John was forging ahead at this point while we kept up the rear and when a solitary girl appeared from the opposite direction with a dog running behind her I flagged her down and asked about the route to the glacier. She was an English speaking local resident and immediately gave us the bald facts saying, "I wouldn't go up there today. There's another storm coming in and once it hits the glacier it will funnel its way down to the valley below like a steam train - with more danger to remaining trees."

We stopped in our tracks at this information then hastened to catch up on John to see what he thought, but his opinion was to forge ahead as far as possible, although he conceded that plans could change if there was a deterioration. Heather wanted to go down right away but was coaxed into continuing until the position became more relevant. At that stage the trees were blocking out some of the view above and the steep slopes of the hill were sheltering us from the wind. The prize for forging ahead was the sight of the glacier below and neighbouring peaks, then suddenly, just as we caught sight of the Montenvers Hotel there was an almighty blast from below, like an explosion from a quarry. "Whatever was that?" We jumped in fright.

I wondered if it was the foresters blasting trees off the mountain railway, but the girls thought it was an avalanche, while John was too far ahead again to profess his opinion.

As Montenvers was so close we carried on somewhat shaken, meeting up with John as the force of the wind suddenly hit us out in the open. We linked arms and staggered over to the wall between the hotel and the train station, where we could look down onto the Mer de Glace far below. Surprisingly the pinnacles on the far side were almost clear of mist, leering upwards in intimidating, sheer icy sweeps against the brooding, grey sky, spelling out the approach of winter - Aiguille du Dru, les Droites, and Aiguille Verte.

The girls were unimpressed as they battled to keep their feet in the wind and we could hear it roaring below as it gathered speed across the glacier, where the ice was shrouded in grey moraine dust and debris. We hung onto each other as we sidled along the wall, making our way back towards the relative shelter of the funicular train station. The blasting wind was trying to uproot everything that wasn't nailed down, but when we rounded a corner we stumbled upon two railway workers eating their lunch!

Heather spoke to them in French and reported that they had said we were very brave coming up here on a day like this! We thought so too actually, until we bumped into a few more stalwart walkers heading for a bird's eye view of the glacier. So - there were other brave people about, all of them wanting to see the devastation and sights for themselves. This boosted our morale and as we descended and reached the shelter of the remaining forest we felt pleased with our achievement and made good time back to Chamonix.

John was inclined to look upon the expedition as an adventure, while I was slightly less enamoured and the girls were relieved to regain the sanctuary of the chalet.

However, the shocks and surprises were not over yet, because when we returned to Calais two days later we discovered there had been equal devastation in the south of England, where the storm that had swept through Chamonix had landed in Kent the day before our arrival. Not having read any newspapers on holiday we were unaware of all this and had a long wait for a functioning ferry in the departure lounge at Calais, followed by mayhem at Dover on the other side. The south east and most of London had been blacked out as power lines came down and no trains were running, leaving us to cram into buses for the evening journey back to Victoria in pitch darkness. Not since World War Two had there been devastation on such a humungous scale it was reported in the press. We decided it was the last time we were going on holiday abroad in October!